Agile Project Management: Navigating Change with Confidence

No part of this publication may be reproduced, distributed, or transmitted in any form or by any means, including photocopying, recording, or other electronic or mechanical methods, without the prior written permission of the publisher, except in the case of brief quotations embodied in critical reviews and certain other noncommercial uses permitted by copyright law.

Copyright © 2024 Infowave MRV
All rights reserved.

Table of Content:

Chapter 1: Introduction to Agile Project Management

- Overview of Agile principles and values.
- Importance of Agile in today's dynamic business environment.

Chapter 2: The Agile Manifesto

- Deep dive into the four values and twelve principles of the Agile Manifesto.
- Implications for project management practices.

Chapter 3: Key Agile Frameworks

- Overview of popular Agile frameworks (Scrum, Kanban, Lean, etc.).
- When to use each framework based on project needs.

Chapter 4: The Role of the Agile Project Manager

- Responsibilities and skills of an Agile project manager.
- Leadership styles in an Agile environment.

Chapter 5: Building Agile Teams

- Characteristics of high-performing Agile teams.
- Strategies for team formation and development.

Chapter 6: User Stories and Backlog Management

- Crafting effective user stories.
- Prioritizing and managing the product backlog.

Chapter 7: Sprint Planning and Execution

- Key activities in sprint planning.
- Best practices for executing sprints successfully.

Chapter 8: Daily Stand-ups and Team Collaboration

- Importance of daily stand-ups in fostering communication.
- Techniques for enhancing team collaboration.

Chapter 9: Measuring Progress and Success

- Metrics and KPIs for Agile projects.
- Tools for tracking progress (burn-down charts, etc.).

Chapter 10: Adapting to Change

- Embracing change as a core principle of Agile.
- Strategies for managing changing requirements.

Chapter 11: Agile Risk Management

- Identifying and assessing risks in Agile projects.
- Techniques for mitigating risks in an Agile context.

Chapter 12: Stakeholder Engagement

- Importance of stakeholder involvement in Agile.
- Strategies for effective communication and collaboration.

Chapter 13: Agile Quality Assurance

- Integrating quality assurance into Agile processes.
- Continuous testing and feedback loops.

Chapter 14: Scaling Agile

- Challenges and strategies for scaling Agile practices.
- Overview of frameworks for scaling Agile (SAFe, LeSS, etc.).

Chapter 15: Agile Tools and Technologies

- Tools to facilitate Agile project management (JIRA, Trello, etc.).
- How technology can enhance Agile practices.

Chapter 16: Agile Mindset and Culture

- Fostering an Agile mindset within teams and organizations.
- Cultural changes needed for Agile success.

Chapter 17: Case Studies in Agile Project Management

- Real-world examples of successful Agile projects.
- Lessons learned from Agile implementations.

Chapter 18: Common Challenges in Agile Adoption

- Typical pitfalls and challenges organizations face.
- Strategies for overcoming resistance to Agile.

Chapter 19: The Future of Agile Project Management

- Emerging trends and the evolving landscape of Agile.
- Predictions for the future of project management.

Chapter 20: Conclusion: Navigating Change with Confidence

- Recap of key concepts.
- Encouragement for readers to embrace Agile practices in their projects.

Chapter 1: Introduction to Agile Project Management

In today's fast-paced and constantly evolving business landscape, organizations face increasing pressure to deliver results quickly while remaining adaptable to change. Traditional project management methodologies, which often rely on rigid planning and sequential execution, can struggle to meet these demands. Enter Agile project management — a dynamic and flexible approach designed to empower teams, embrace change, and deliver value iteratively.

In this chapter, we'll explore the foundational elements of Agile project management, explain why it has become such a popular choice for organizations, and set the stage for a deeper dive into Agile methodologies and practices.

What Is Agile Project Management?

Agile project management is an iterative approach to planning and guiding project processes. Unlike traditional "waterfall" methodologies, which rely on upfront planning and linear execution, Agile breaks projects into small, manageable increments called iterations or sprints. This allows for constant feedback, adaptation, and improvement.

At its core, Agile prioritizes collaboration, flexibility, and customer satisfaction. Agile teams work closely with stakeholders, frequently delivering usable products, and continuously refining based on feedback. Agile's adaptability makes it particularly effective in environments where project requirements evolve over time, which is common in software development, but also increasingly relevant across various industries.

The Shift from Traditional to Agile

Traditional project management methods, such as the Waterfall approach, emphasize a structured sequence of phases: requirements gathering, design, development, testing, and deployment. Each phase must be completed before moving to the next, and changes can be difficult to incorporate once the project is underway.

While this approach works well for projects with fixed requirements, it presents challenges when dealing with uncertainty, change, or complex user needs. Imagine developing software for a client who changes their mind about critical features halfway through the project. In a Waterfall model, this would likely mean going back to the drawing board, incurring delays and increased costs.

Agile, on the other hand, embraces change as part of the process. By delivering work in small increments, it allows teams to adjust course based on feedback from customers, stakeholders, or evolving market conditions. This ensures that the end product remains aligned with the user's needs, even if those needs change over time.

Why Agile Is Gaining Popularity

Several factors contribute to the widespread adoption of Agile project management:

1. Flexibility and Adaptability: Agile allows for changes in project scope, requirements, and priorities, making it ideal for fast-moving industries where responsiveness is key.

2. Continuous Delivery of Value: Rather than waiting until the end of a project to deliver the final product, Agile teams deliver usable versions (or increments) of the product regularly. This ensures that stakeholders can see progress and provide feedback throughout the development process.

3. Improved Collaboration and Communication: Agile promotes frequent communication between teams and stakeholders. Daily stand-up meetings, sprint reviews, and retrospectives keep everyone aligned and engaged.

4. Risk Mitigation: Agile's incremental nature reduces risk by identifying potential problems early and allowing for course corrections before they become significant issues. This "fail fast" mentality helps teams learn quickly and improve continuously.

5. Enhanced Customer Satisfaction: With Agile, customer feedback is integrated throughout the development process. This leads to products that are more closely aligned with user needs, ultimately resulting in higher customer satisfaction.

Agile Values and Principles

At the heart of Agile project management lies the Agile Manifesto, which was created in 2001 by a group of software developers seeking a better way to manage projects. The Agile Manifesto outlines four core values and twelve guiding principles, which have since become the foundation of Agile practices.

The Four Values of the Agile Manifesto:

1. **Individuals and interactions over processes and tools:** Agile places more emphasis on people and communication rather than rigid adherence to processes or reliance on tools.
2. **Working software over comprehensive documentation:** While documentation is important, delivering a working product is the top priority. In non-software contexts, this means focusing on delivering a tangible result rather than excessive planning.
3. **Customer collaboration over contract negotiation:** Agile encourages ongoing collaboration with customers and stakeholders

throughout the project, ensuring that their needs are met as they evolve.
4. **Responding to change over following a plan:** Agile acknowledges that changes are inevitable and should be welcomed. Rather than sticking to a predefined plan, Agile teams adapt as necessary.

The Twelve Principles of Agile:

1. **Customer satisfaction through early and continuous delivery of valuable work.**
2. **Welcome changing requirements, even late in development.**
3. **Deliver working products frequently, with a preference for shorter timescales.**
4. **Businesspeople and developers must work together daily throughout the project.**
5. **Build projects around motivated individuals, giving them the environment and support they need.**
6. **Face-to-face communication is the most effective way to convey information.**
7. **Working software is the primary measure of progress.**
8. **Agile processes promote sustainable development, maintaining a constant pace indefinitely.**
9. **Continuous attention to technical excellence and good design enhances agility.**

10. **Simplicity—the art of maximizing the amount of work not done—is essential.**
11. **The best architectures, requirements, and designs emerge from self-organizing teams.**
12. **At regular intervals, the team reflects on how to become more effective and adjusts accordingly.**

Key Benefits of Agile

Let's take a closer look at some of the most compelling benefits that Agile brings to project management:

- **Faster Time to Market:** By delivering smaller increments of the product, teams can bring usable features or products to market faster, gaining a competitive edge.
- **Increased Flexibility:** Agile's iterative nature allows teams to respond to feedback and adjust their approach quickly without disrupting the overall project.
- **Enhanced Product Quality:** Agile promotes continuous testing and integration, ensuring that issues are caught and addressed early in the development cycle.
- **Greater Stakeholder Engagement:** Regular feedback loops with stakeholders keep everyone on the same page and aligned with the project's goals.

- **Higher Team Morale:** Agile emphasizes team collaboration and empowerment, creating an environment where team members feel valued and motivated.

When to Use Agile

While Agile offers numerous benefits, it's not a one-size-fits-all solution. Agile is most effective in projects where:

- **Requirements are likely to change** over time due to evolving customer needs or market conditions.
- **The end product is complex** and may require ongoing iteration and refinement.
- **Customer involvement is high,** and frequent feedback is desired.
- **The team is self-motivated, collaborative,** and empowered to make decisions.

Agile may not be as effective in projects where requirements are fixed from the outset, or where regulatory or compliance constraints require detailed upfront planning.

Conclusion

Agile project management is a game-changer for organizations that operate in environments characterized by rapid change, uncertainty, and evolving customer expectations. By prioritizing collaboration, flexibility, and continuous improvement, Agile empowers teams to navigate complexity with confidence and deliver high-quality products that meet customer needs.

As we move forward in this book, we'll explore the specific practices, tools, and techniques that bring Agile to life. From understanding the Agile frameworks to mastering the art of sprint planning, you'll gain the knowledge needed to successfully implement Agile in your own projects.

In the next chapter, we'll dive deeper into the **Agile Manifesto**, exploring the values and principles that form the foundation of this transformative approach to project management.

Chapter 2: The Agile Manifesto

The Agile Manifesto is the foundation of Agile project management. Created in 2001 by a group of software developers who were dissatisfied with traditional project management methodologies, it offers a fresh perspective on managing projects in a rapidly changing environment. The Agile Manifesto isn't just for software development; its values and principles have been widely adopted across various industries. In this chapter, we'll explore the origins, values, and guiding principles of the Agile Manifesto, helping you understand why it's so influential and how it can transform your approach to managing projects.

The Birth of the Agile Manifesto

In February 2001, 17 software development experts gathered at a ski resort in Snowbird, Utah, with a mission: to find a better way of managing projects. They were frustrated by the limitations of traditional project management methodologies, particularly the Waterfall method, which often led to long development cycles, costly changes, and misaligned products. Their solution? A new framework that prioritized flexibility, customer collaboration, and responsiveness to change. This framework became known as Agile.

The group published their conclusions in what is now called the **Agile Manifesto**, a brief document that outlines the core values and principles of Agile project management. It serves as a philosophical guide, helping teams adopt a mindset that values people, results, and adaptability over rigid processes and documentation.

The Four Core Values of the Agile Manifesto

At the heart of the Agile Manifesto are four core values. These values highlight the key differences between Agile and traditional project management approaches. They are not meant to completely discard traditional methods but rather to shift priorities towards a more adaptive and customer-focused approach.

1. Individuals and Interactions over Processes and Tools

This value emphasizes the importance of communication and collaboration among team members. In traditional project management, there is often a heavy reliance on tools, formal processes, and documentation to manage projects. While tools and processes have their place, Agile stresses that people and their interactions are more critical to project success.

Agile teams focus on daily communication, brainstorming, and decision-making as a group. This fosters creativity, problem-solving, and a shared sense of ownership. A tool cannot replace the value of face-to-face discussions or spontaneous problem-solving moments.

2. Working Software over Comprehensive Documentation

In traditional project management, extensive documentation is often created before any work begins. This documentation can include everything from detailed requirement specifications to lengthy project plans. While documentation is important, Agile believes that delivering a functional product is far more valuable than spending too much time documenting every step of the process.

Agile teams aim to deliver working increments of the product frequently, which allows stakeholders to provide feedback early and often. The focus is on developing software (or any deliverable) that adds value, rather than producing paperwork that may never be referenced.

3. Customer Collaboration over Contract Negotiation

Traditional project management often revolves around formal contracts that dictate the scope, timeline, and cost of a project. Once the contract is signed, changes to the project can be difficult and expensive to manage. Agile shifts the focus to continuous collaboration with the customer or client. Instead of rigidly adhering to an initial contract, Agile encourages frequent check-ins and feedback to ensure that the product aligns with the customer's evolving needs. This collaborative approach creates a partnership between the team and the customer, leading to better outcomes and more satisfied clients.

4. Responding to Change over Following a Plan
One of the major criticisms of traditional project management is its inflexibility. Teams often create detailed plans at the beginning of a project, only to find that the market or customer needs have shifted midway through development. Agile recognizes that change is inevitable and should be embraced rather than resisted. In Agile, planning is done continuously, not just at the beginning. Teams adapt their plans based on feedback, new information, or changing circumstances. The goal is to remain flexible and responsive, ensuring that the project delivers maximum value even if the initial plan changes.

The Twelve Principles of Agile

In addition to the four core values, the Agile Manifesto outlines twelve guiding principles. These principles provide more detailed guidance on how Agile should be practiced in day-to-day project management. Let's explore each one:

1. Our highest priority is to satisfy the customer through early and continuous delivery of valuable software.
Agile teams strive to deliver usable products early in the project and keep delivering value throughout the process. This ensures that the customer remains engaged and satisfied with the project's progress.

2. Welcome changing requirements, even late in development. Agile processes harness change for the customer's competitive advantage.

Change is not seen as a setback but as an opportunity. Agile teams are prepared to adapt to new requirements, even if they arise late in the development cycle, to ensure that the final product meets the customer's needs.

3. Deliver working software frequently, from a couple of weeks to a couple of months, with a preference for the shorter timescale.

By delivering working software (or product increments) frequently, teams can gather feedback and make adjustments early in the project, reducing the risk of failure.

4. Businesspeople and developers must work together daily throughout the project.

Agile promotes close collaboration between the technical team and business stakeholders. This ensures that the team understands the business goals and that the product aligns with customer expectations.

5. Build projects around motivated individuals. Give them the environment and support they need, and trust them to get the job done.

Agile emphasizes the importance of trust and empowerment. Team members should be motivated and given the resources they need to succeed, without being micromanaged.

6. The most efficient and effective method of conveying information to and within a development team is face-to-face conversation.
While digital tools are useful, Agile promotes in-person (or video-based) communication as the best way to ensure clarity and understanding.

7. Working software is the primary measure of progress.
In Agile, the success of a project is measured by how much value has been delivered through working software (or products), not by how much documentation has been completed or how closely the project follows a predetermined plan.

8. Agile processes promote sustainable development. The sponsors, developers, and users should be able to maintain a constant pace indefinitely.
Agile discourages overwork and burnout. Instead, it promotes a sustainable work pace that ensures long-term productivity and team well-being.

9. Continuous attention to technical excellence and good design enhances agility.
Agile teams focus on technical excellence and good design practices to ensure that their products are flexible, maintainable, and scalable.

10. Simplicity—the art of maximizing the amount of work not done—is essential.
Agile values simplicity. Teams should avoid unnecessary features or complexity, focusing instead on delivering the most critical features with the highest impact.

11. The best architectures, requirements, and designs emerge from self-organizing teams.
Agile teams are self-organizing, meaning that they determine how best to accomplish their work without needing external direction. This autonomy fosters creativity and innovation.

12. At regular intervals, the team reflects on how to become more effective, then tunes and adjusts its behavior accordingly.
Agile encourages continuous improvement. Teams regularly review their performance and identify ways to improve their processes and collaboration.

The Importance of Mindset in Agile

Adopting Agile is more than just following processes and techniques. It's about embracing a mindset that prioritizes flexibility, collaboration, and customer value. The Agile Manifesto and its twelve principles guide teams toward this mindset, but the real transformation happens when individuals and organizations internalize these values.

An Agile mindset encourages teams to:

- **Be adaptable:** Recognize that change is inevitable, and be prepared to pivot when necessary.
- **Focus on value:** Always ask, "What will deliver the most value to the customer right now?"
- **Collaborate openly:** Foster a culture of open communication and shared responsibility.
- **Seek continuous improvement:** Never be satisfied with the status quo—always look for ways to improve processes, skills, and outcomes.

Conclusion

The Agile Manifesto provides the philosophical foundation for Agile project management. Its values and principles emphasize flexibility, collaboration, and a relentless focus on delivering value to the customer. By embracing these values, teams can better navigate the complexities of modern project management, respond to change, and build products that truly meet their customers' needs.

In the next chapter, we'll explore the key Agile frameworks, including Scrum, Kanban, and Lean, and how they put these values and principles into practice.

Chapter 3: Key Agile Frameworks

Agile is more than just a mindset; it's a collection of practices and methodologies that help teams bring its values and principles to life. These practices, often referred to as Agile frameworks, provide structured approaches for managing projects, fostering collaboration, and delivering value incrementally. In this chapter, we'll dive deep into the most widely used Agile frameworks: Scrum, Kanban, and Lean. Each of these frameworks offers unique benefits and can be tailored to fit different types of projects, industries, and team dynamics.

What Are Agile Frameworks?

Agile frameworks are structured methods that teams use to implement Agile principles in their projects. While the Agile Manifesto provides the guiding philosophy, frameworks like Scrum and Kanban offer practical tools, processes, and roles for managing work. These frameworks aren't rigid; they're adaptable, and teams often mix and match elements to suit their specific needs.

The three most popular Agile frameworks we will explore in this chapter are:

1. Scrum
2. Kanban
3. Lean

Each framework offers a different way of managing tasks, coordinating teams, and delivering value, but all are rooted in Agile principles like adaptability, collaboration, and iterative development.

Scrum

Overview
Scrum is one of the most widely used Agile frameworks. It's designed for teams that need a structured approach to managing complex projects, typically in a dynamic environment where requirements may change frequently. Scrum is built around short, time-boxed periods called **sprints**, which usually last between one and four weeks. During each sprint, teams focus on delivering a usable increment of the product.

Core Components of Scrum
Scrum has a defined set of roles, events, and artifacts, which provide structure to the development process while allowing for flexibility and collaboration.

1. Scrum Roles

Scrum defines three primary roles that are essential to the framework:

- **Product Owner**: The Product Owner is responsible for representing the interests of the stakeholders and ensuring that the team is working on the most valuable features. They manage the product backlog, prioritize tasks, and collaborate closely with the team to provide clarity on what needs to be built.
- **Scrum Master**: The Scrum Master acts as a facilitator, ensuring that the team follows Scrum practices and resolves any impediments that may block the team's progress. They are responsible for fostering an environment of collaboration and continuous improvement.
- **Development Team**: The development team is a cross-functional group of professionals responsible for delivering the product. They are empowered to decide how to accomplish their work within each sprint and are self-organizing, meaning they determine the best way to complete their tasks without relying on external direction.

2. Scrum Events

Scrum operates on a rhythm of regular events designed to facilitate planning, collaboration, and review.

- **Sprint**: The sprint is the heartbeat of Scrum. It is a time-boxed period (usually two to four weeks) during which the team works on a specific set of features or tasks from the product backlog. At the end of the sprint, the team delivers a potentially shippable product increment.
- **Sprint Planning**: At the start of each sprint, the team holds a sprint planning meeting to decide what work will be completed during the sprint. The Product Owner presents the prioritized tasks from the product backlog, and the development team selects what they can realistically complete within the sprint.
- **Daily Standup (Daily Scrum)**: Every day, the team holds a brief stand-up meeting to discuss progress, share updates, and identify any obstacles. This meeting ensures that everyone is aligned and can address potential issues quickly.
- **Sprint Review**: At the end of the sprint, the team holds a sprint review to demonstrate the completed work to stakeholders and receive feedback. This feedback is essential for ensuring that the product remains aligned with user needs and business goals.
- **Sprint Retrospective**: After the sprint review, the team holds a sprint retrospective to reflect on what went well and what could be improved. This meeting encourages continuous improvement and helps the team refine their processes.

3. Scrum Artifacts
Scrum uses several key artifacts to help manage work and track progress:

- **Product Backlog**: The product backlog is a prioritized list of features, enhancements, bug fixes, and other tasks that need to be completed. The Product Owner manages this list, ensuring that the most important tasks are at the top.
- **Sprint Backlog**: The sprint backlog is a subset of the product backlog that the development team commits to completing during a sprint. It is created during the sprint planning meeting and represents the team's immediate goals.
- **Increment**: The increment is the working product delivered at the end of each sprint. It should be in a usable state, even if it's not the final version, allowing stakeholders to review it and provide feedback.

Why Scrum Works
Scrum works well because it breaks complex projects into manageable chunks, allows for continuous feedback, and promotes collaboration between teams and stakeholders. The time-boxed nature of sprints keeps the team focused, while the regular review and retrospective sessions ensure that the team is always learning and improving.

Kanban

Overview

Kanban is another popular Agile framework that focuses on visualizing work, limiting work-in-progress, and continuously improving efficiency. Unlike Scrum, which operates in defined sprints, Kanban is a continuous flow system. This makes it ideal for teams that need to manage ongoing work without the need for fixed iterations.

Core Components of Kanban

Kanban is built around the concept of a **Kanban board**, which provides a visual representation of the work being done. The board is typically divided into columns, with each column representing a different stage in the workflow, such as "To Do," "In Progress," and "Done."

1. Visualizing Workflow

One of the key strengths of Kanban is its focus on visualizing work. By representing each task as a card on the Kanban board, the entire team can see the current status of each task at a glance. This transparency helps teams identify bottlenecks, optimize their workflow, and ensure that work is evenly distributed.

2. Limiting Work in Progress (WIP)

Kanban emphasizes limiting the amount of work in progress at any given time. By setting a WIP limit for each stage of the workflow, teams can prevent themselves from overcommitting and ensure that they complete tasks before starting new ones. This leads to more efficient work and better quality output.

3. Continuous Improvement
Kanban encourages teams to focus on continuously improving their process. By regularly reviewing the flow of work and identifying areas for optimization, teams can reduce delays, eliminate inefficiencies, and improve their overall performance.

Kanban vs. Scrum
While both Kanban and Scrum are Agile frameworks, they differ in several key ways. Scrum is based on time-boxed sprints and clearly defined roles and events, while Kanban is more flexible and focuses on visualizing work and limiting WIP. Scrum is ideal for teams working on projects with well-defined goals, while Kanban works well for teams with a continuous flow of work.

Lean

Overview
Lean is an Agile framework rooted in the manufacturing industry, particularly in Toyota's production system. However, its principles have been widely adapted for use in software development and other industries. Lean focuses on maximizing customer value by minimizing waste. This framework encourages teams to streamline

their processes, eliminate inefficiencies, and deliver value as quickly as possible.

Core Principles of Lean

Lean is based on several key principles that guide teams toward creating more value with fewer resources:

1. Eliminate Waste

Lean teams are constantly looking for ways to eliminate waste, which can take many forms, such as unnecessary features, rework, or inefficient processes. By focusing only on activities that add value to the customer, teams can reduce costs, improve quality, and accelerate delivery.

2. Amplify Learning

In Lean, continuous learning is essential for improvement. Teams are encouraged to experiment, gather feedback, and adapt based on what they learn. This approach ensures that the product is always evolving to meet customer needs.

3. Build Quality In

Lean teams aim to build quality into their processes from the start, rather than relying on inspections or testing to catch defects later. This reduces the need for rework and ensures that the final product meets the customer's expectations.

4. Deliver Fast

Lean prioritizes delivering value to the customer as

quickly as possible. By breaking work into smaller increments and continuously delivering them, Lean teams can respond to customer needs faster and more effectively.

5. Empower the Team
Lean encourages teams to be self-organizing and autonomous. Teams are given the responsibility to make decisions about how to accomplish their work, leading to more creative solutions and a stronger sense of ownership.

6. Respect People
Respect for people is a core tenet of Lean. This means creating a culture of trust, collaboration, and continuous improvement. Lean teams recognize that people are the most valuable resource, and their insights and creativity are essential to success.

7. Optimize the Whole
Lean teams take a holistic view of the project, ensuring that the entire process is optimized, not just individual parts. This ensures that improvements in one area don't create inefficiencies in another.

Choosing the Right Framework

Selecting the right Agile framework depends on your project's needs, your team's dynamics, and the goals of the organization. Scrum works well for teams that need structure and regular feedback loops, while Kanban is ideal for teams that want to focus on flow and continuous improvement. Lean, with its focus on eliminating waste and maximizing value, is perfect for teams looking to streamline their processes and deliver value faster.

Many teams adopt a hybrid approach, combining elements from multiple frameworks to create a customized Agile process that best suits their unique challenges.

Conclusion

The Agile frameworks of Scrum, Kanban, and Lean each offer valuable tools for implementing Agile principles in project management. By understanding the strengths and differences of each framework, teams can choose the best approach for their specific context, allowing them to deliver value faster, collaborate more effectively, and adapt to change with greater ease.

In the next chapter, we will explore the concept of Agile roles in more detail, focusing on how these roles contribute to successful project outcomes and the responsibilities each team member has in an Agile environment.

Chapter 4: The Role of the Agile Project Manager

In traditional project management, the project manager plays a central role in planning, executing, and controlling the entire project. However, Agile methodologies introduce a different approach to managing projects, one that emphasizes self-organizing teams, flexibility, and collaboration. The role of the Agile Project Manager is less about directing and more about facilitating, coaching, and ensuring that the team is empowered to succeed. In this chapter, we will explore the key responsibilities and functions of the Agile Project Manager and how this role differs from traditional project management.

The Evolving Role of the Project Manager in Agile

In Agile, the concept of "project management" shifts. Rather than being the sole decision-maker or the person responsible for every aspect of the project, the Agile Project Manager focuses on creating an environment where the team can thrive. Agile encourages shared responsibility, meaning that teams are self-organizing, empowered to make decisions, and accountable for delivering results. The Agile Project Manager's role is to support this process by removing obstacles, fostering collaboration, and helping the team stay aligned with the project goals.

Agile Project Managers also work closely with other roles like the Scrum Master and Product Owner in frameworks like Scrum, ensuring that all pieces of the Agile process come together effectively.

Key Responsibilities of the Agile Project Manager

1. Facilitating Communication and Collaboration
One of the primary responsibilities of an Agile Project Manager is to ensure that communication flows smoothly between all stakeholders—team members, customers, and other departments. In Agile, transparency and frequent communication are essential for success. The Agile Project Manager fosters a collaborative environment by encouraging open dialogue, promoting cross-functional teamwork, and ensuring that everyone is aligned on project goals.

Regular meetings, such as daily stand-ups, sprint reviews, and retrospectives, are often facilitated by the Agile Project Manager to ensure that the team is communicating effectively, sharing knowledge, and making decisions collectively. However, the Agile Project Manager is not the sole leader of these meetings; they may delegate or share the responsibility with the Scrum Master or other team members.

2. Removing Obstacles (Impediments)
A critical part of the Agile Project Manager's role is removing obstacles that may slow down or block the

team's progress. These impediments can range from resource shortages, technical issues, or even team dynamics that hinder productivity. The Agile Project Manager works proactively to identify potential risks and bottlenecks and collaborates with the team to remove them.

For example, if a team is facing challenges due to a lack of clarity around customer requirements, the Agile Project Manager can facilitate discussions with the Product Owner to ensure the team has the information they need. If external dependencies are slowing down the work, the Agile Project Manager coordinates with other teams or departments to resolve those issues.

3. Facilitating Agile Practices and Processes

Agile teams rely on structured processes, such as sprint planning, backlog refinement, and retrospectives, to stay organized and maintain momentum. The Agile Project Manager helps ensure that these practices are followed correctly while remaining adaptable to the team's needs.

In frameworks like Scrum, the Scrum Master often takes on the responsibility of facilitating Agile events, but the Agile Project Manager may also support this process, especially if the organization doesn't have a designated Scrum Master. They ensure that meetings remain productive, focused, and aligned with Agile principles. However, the Agile Project Manager should avoid micromanaging the team or dictating how they should work. The goal is to empower the team to take ownership of these processes.

4. Aligning the Team with Project Vision and Goals
One of the main responsibilities of the Agile Project Manager is to keep the team aligned with the project vision and objectives. In Agile projects, priorities can change frequently based on customer feedback or market conditions. It's the Agile Project Manager's job to ensure that the team understands the project's current priorities and how their work fits into the bigger picture.

This involves close collaboration with the Product Owner, who is responsible for defining the product backlog and prioritizing features. The Agile Project Manager helps translate these priorities into actionable tasks for the team while ensuring that everyone remains focused on delivering value to the customer.

5. Encouraging Continuous Improvement
Agile emphasizes continuous improvement through frequent reflection and adaptation. The Agile Project Manager plays an important role in promoting a culture of learning and growth within the team. After each sprint or iteration, the team holds a retrospective to discuss what went well and what could be improved. The Agile Project Manager facilitates these discussions, encouraging the team to identify opportunities for

improvement and implement changes that enhance productivity, collaboration, or quality.

The Agile Project Manager also encourages individual team members to improve their skills, whether by providing learning opportunities, encouraging experimentation, or promoting cross-functional training. By fostering a mindset of continuous learning, the Agile Project Manager helps the team evolve and stay competitive in a fast-changing environment.

6. Managing Stakeholder Expectations
Agile projects involve frequent interactions with stakeholders to ensure that the product being developed meets their needs. The Agile Project Manager acts as a bridge between the team and the stakeholders, ensuring that expectations are managed appropriately. This means keeping stakeholders informed about the team's progress, potential risks, and any changes in scope.

In Agile, stakeholders are often closely involved in the development process, providing feedback on iterations of the product. The Agile Project Manager ensures that this feedback loop remains active and productive. They also manage any conflicts or misalignments between stakeholders' expectations and the team's capacity, ensuring that realistic goals are set and that the project remains on track.

7. Supporting a Self-Organizing Team

Agile teams are self-organizing, meaning they have the autonomy to decide how they will approach their work and solve problems. The Agile Project Manager supports this autonomy by providing guidance without controlling or dictating every decision. Instead of telling the team what to do, the Agile Project Manager creates an environment where the team can collaborate, make decisions, and find creative solutions.

Supporting self-organizing teams also involves building trust. The Agile Project Manager should trust the team's expertise and judgment, giving them the space to experiment, fail, learn, and succeed. By encouraging empowerment and ownership, the Agile Project Manager helps the team become more effective and engaged.

The Agile Project Manager vs. Scrum Master

It's important to differentiate between the role of the Agile Project Manager and the Scrum Master, especially in Scrum-based teams. While both roles share similar responsibilities in supporting the team and facilitating Agile practices, they are distinct in their focus and scope.

- **Scrum Master**: The Scrum Master focuses specifically on Scrum practices and the team's adherence to the Scrum framework. Their role is

more of a coach and process facilitator, ensuring that the team follows Scrum principles and events like sprint planning, daily stand-ups, and retrospectives. The Scrum Master doesn't typically engage with external stakeholders or manage the broader project beyond the Scrum team.
- **Agile Project Manager**: The Agile Project Manager, on the other hand, has a broader focus. They not only facilitate Agile processes but also engage with stakeholders, manage external dependencies, and provide strategic guidance to the team. They may work across multiple teams and frameworks, depending on the organization's needs.

In some organizations, both roles exist separately, while in others, the responsibilities may overlap or be combined depending on the team's size and structure.

Empowering the Team for Success

Ultimately, the Agile Project Manager's role is about empowerment. Instead of managing every detail, they provide the team with the tools, support, and environment needed to succeed. This includes fostering collaboration, removing roadblocks, facilitating Agile processes, and ensuring that the team remains aligned with the project's goals and vision.

The shift from traditional project management to Agile can be challenging for those used to controlling every aspect of a project. However, by embracing a servant-leadership approach, Agile Project Managers can help their teams become more autonomous, collaborative, and productive.

Conclusion

The Agile Project Manager plays a vital role in ensuring the success of Agile projects, but their responsibilities are more about facilitation and support than direct control. By fostering communication, removing impediments, encouraging continuous improvement, and empowering the team to self-organize, Agile Project Managers help teams deliver value in a dynamic, customer-focused environment.

In the next chapter, we will explore how to build and manage a high-performing Agile team, focusing on the skills, roles, and dynamics that contribute to success.

Chapter 5: Building Agile Teams

In Agile, the success of any project heavily relies on the strength and effectiveness of the team. Unlike traditional teams, where roles and responsibilities are rigidly defined, Agile teams are cross-functional, self-organizing, and highly collaborative. Building an Agile team requires not only the right mix of skills but also fostering a culture of trust, adaptability, and continuous improvement. In this chapter, we will explore the key components of an Agile team, the essential roles within the team, and the qualities that make an Agile team thrive.

The Importance of Cross-Functionality in Agile Teams

A defining characteristic of Agile teams is their cross-functionality. This means that team members possess a diverse range of skills, allowing them to handle all aspects of product development. In traditional project management, different departments or specialized teams often handle tasks like design, development, and testing. Agile eliminates this siloed approach, bringing together individuals with varied expertise into a single team.

Cross-functional teams increase flexibility and reduce dependencies. For example, an Agile team working on software development might include developers, testers, designers, and product managers. By having all necessary skills within the team, they can move faster, collaborate more effectively, and adapt quickly to changes.

Each team member contributes their expertise, but they are also encouraged to learn new skills outside their core discipline. This creates a more versatile team where everyone can contribute to multiple areas of the project, enhancing the team's ability to respond to changing requirements or challenges.

Self-Organizing Teams

Another key attribute of Agile teams is that they are self-organizing. Rather than having a traditional manager dictate who does what, the team collaboratively decides how best to approach the work. Team members take ownership of their tasks, share responsibilities, and make decisions collectively.

Self-organizing teams are empowered to experiment with different ways of working. This autonomy enables them to innovate and find the most efficient methods to achieve project goals. It also fosters accountability, as team members are responsible not only for their individual tasks but also for the overall success of the project.

For this model to work effectively, there needs to be a high level of trust and mutual respect among team members. The Agile Project Manager or Scrum Master plays a crucial role in fostering this environment by removing obstacles, facilitating communication, and encouraging collaboration, without micromanaging the team.

Key Roles in an Agile Team

While Agile teams are self-organizing and cross-functional, there are still specific roles that guide the process and ensure that the team functions smoothly. These roles vary slightly depending on the Agile framework (such as Scrum or Kanban), but the following are common roles within most Agile teams:

1. Product Owner
The Product Owner is the voice of the customer and is responsible for maximizing the value delivered by the team. They manage the product backlog, prioritize tasks, and define the product vision and goals. The Product Owner works closely with stakeholders to gather requirements and ensure that the team is always focused on delivering what matters most to the customer.

2. Scrum Master or Agile Coach
The Scrum Master (in Scrum) or Agile Coach (in other Agile frameworks) is responsible for ensuring that the team follows Agile principles and practices. They facilitate meetings, remove impediments, and help the team continuously improve. The Scrum Master or Agile

Coach also acts as a coach, guiding the team in its journey toward self-organization and high performance.

3. Team Members (Developers, Designers, Testers, etc.)

In Agile, team members are often referred to simply as "developers," but this can include anyone involved in the creation of the product, such as software engineers, designers, quality assurance testers, and business analysts. Team members collaborate closely, share knowledge, and take collective ownership of delivering high-quality results. Because Agile teams are cross-functional, these team members may work across different areas of the project, and they are encouraged to continuously expand their skills.

4. Stakeholders

Although not part of the Agile team itself, stakeholders play a crucial role in guiding the project's direction. Stakeholders can include customers, business leaders, and other external parties with a vested interest in the project's success. They provide valuable feedback, help shape the product vision, and collaborate with the Product Owner to ensure that the team delivers value.

Creating a Collaborative and Trusting Environment

The strength of an Agile team lies in its ability to collaborate effectively. To achieve this, team members must feel comfortable sharing ideas, giving and receiving feedback, and working together to solve problems. Creating a collaborative culture requires establishing trust, transparency, and open communication.

1. Trust and Psychological Safety
Trust is the foundation of any high-performing Agile team. When team members trust one another, they are more willing to take risks, experiment with new ideas, and voice concerns without fear of blame or judgment. Psychological safety—the belief that one can speak up without negative consequences—encourages team members to challenge assumptions, offer creative solutions, and engage in meaningful discussions.

Agile Project Managers or Scrum Masters play a key role in fostering psychological safety by encouraging open dialogue and making sure that every team member's voice is heard. When trust and psychological safety are present, teams can work through conflicts constructively and make better decisions.

2. Transparency
Transparency is a core value in Agile. Teams share progress, challenges, and feedback openly to ensure everyone is aligned and working toward the same goals. Tools like task boards, burndown charts, and sprint backlogs provide visibility into the team's work, allowing everyone to see the current status of the project. This transparency not only improves communication but also

builds accountability, as everyone is aware of the team's progress and can contribute to problem-solving when needed.

3. Regular Feedback and Reflection

Agile teams continuously improve by regularly reflecting on their performance and seeking feedback from stakeholders. Frequent check-ins, such as sprint reviews and retrospectives, provide opportunities for the team to review their progress, celebrate successes, and identify areas for improvement. This focus on continuous improvement keeps the team agile, adaptable, and always moving toward greater efficiency and quality.

Agile Team Dynamics

Building a high-performing Agile team also requires attention to team dynamics. Healthy team dynamics ensure that the group can collaborate effectively, resolve conflicts, and maintain productivity even under pressure.

1. Open Communication

Agile teams thrive on open communication. Regular meetings like daily stand-ups provide a structured space for team members to share progress, discuss challenges, and align on priorities. However, communication shouldn't be limited to formal meetings. Teams should cultivate an environment where members feel free to communicate informally, ask questions, and offer assistance whenever needed.

2. Conflict Resolution

Conflicts are inevitable in any team, especially when working under tight deadlines or navigating complex challenges. Agile teams, however, view conflict as a natural part of collaboration. When handled constructively, conflicts can lead to better solutions and a deeper understanding of different perspectives.

The key to effective conflict resolution is ensuring that team members are comfortable addressing issues openly and respectfully. Agile Project Managers or Scrum Masters can facilitate this process by promoting a culture of healthy debate and helping the team resolve disagreements in a way that strengthens collaboration.

3. Commitment to Shared Goals

Agile teams are united by a common goal: delivering value to the customer. A shared sense of purpose keeps the team focused, motivated, and resilient in the face of challenges. The Agile Project Manager or Product Owner helps maintain this focus by ensuring that the team's work is always aligned with the project's goals and priorities. When everyone is working toward the same objective, the team is more cohesive, engaged, and productive.

Building a Culture of Continuous Improvement

One of the most important characteristics of Agile teams is their commitment to continuous improvement. Agile teams are never satisfied with the status quo; they constantly seek ways to enhance their performance, streamline processes, and deliver more value to the customer.

1. Retrospectives
Retrospectives are a cornerstone of Agile improvement. After each sprint or iteration, the team comes together to reflect on what went well, what didn't, and what can be improved. These regular reflections provide the team with valuable insights into their working methods, allowing them to make small adjustments that lead to long-term improvements.

The Agile Project Manager or Scrum Master facilitates retrospectives, encouraging open, honest discussions and helping the team identify actionable steps for improvement. By fostering a culture of continuous reflection and learning, the team grows stronger and more effective with each sprint.

2. Experimentation and Learning
Agile teams are encouraged to experiment, try new approaches, and learn from both successes and failures. This experimentation fosters innovation and allows teams to discover more efficient ways of working. Agile

Project Managers should encourage this mindset by giving the team the freedom to test new ideas and learn from the outcomes, even if they don't always lead to immediate success.

Conclusion

Building an Agile team requires more than just assembling a group of skilled individuals. It involves creating an environment where collaboration, trust, and continuous improvement are deeply ingrained in the team's culture. By fostering cross-functional skills, supporting self-organization, and encouraging open communication, Agile teams can adapt to changing demands and deliver value with confidence.

Chapter 6: User Stories and Backlog Management

One of the most critical components of Agile project management is the ability to organize, prioritize, and manage work effectively. In Agile, this is done through **user stories** and **backlog management**, which serve as the foundation for planning and executing project tasks. User stories allow teams to capture customer requirements in a simple and understandable format, while backlog management helps ensure that these stories are organized and prioritized based on the value they deliver.

In this chapter, we will dive deep into what user stories are, how to write effective user stories, and how to manage the product backlog in a way that maximizes efficiency and ensures the team is always working on the most important tasks.

Understanding User Stories

At its core, a user story is a short, simple description of a feature or functionality from the perspective of the end user. It focuses on what the user needs and why, rather than how the functionality will be implemented. User stories are written in non-technical language to ensure that everyone, from developers to business stakeholders, understands the requirements.

A typical user story follows a basic format:

As a [user role], I want [desired outcome] so that [benefit].

This format helps keep the focus on the user's needs and the value that the feature will deliver. Let's break it down:

- **User role:** Describes the person who will use the feature (e.g., customer, admin, employee).
- **Desired outcome:** Specifies what the user wants to achieve (e.g., access account details, generate a report).
- **Benefit:** Highlights the reason or value behind the feature (e.g., so that I can track my expenses, so that I can make better business decisions).

For example, a user story might look like this:

As a customer, I want to view my order history so that I can track my previous purchases.

This user story clearly identifies the end user (the customer), the feature they need (viewing order history), and the benefit they expect to gain (tracking previous purchases).

Writing Effective User Stories

While the structure of a user story is simple, writing an effective user story requires a deeper understanding of the user's needs and the context in which the feature will be used. Here are some key principles to keep in mind when writing user stories:

1. Focus on Value to the User
Every user story should emphasize the value it delivers to the user. Rather than focusing on technical specifications, user stories should communicate what the user is trying to achieve. This ensures that the development team understands why the feature is important and how it will impact the user's experience.

2. Keep Stories Small and Actionable
User stories should be small and manageable. Large, complex stories (often referred to as "epics") should be broken down into smaller stories that can be completed within a sprint or iteration. Smaller stories are easier to estimate, prioritize, and implement, leading to more consistent progress.

3. Make Stories Testable
A good user story is testable, meaning that it has clear acceptance criteria that define what "done" looks like. Acceptance criteria outline the conditions that must be met for the story to be considered complete. For

example, in the user story about viewing order history, the acceptance criteria might include:

- The customer can see a list of previous orders.
- Each order shows the date, total amount, and list of items.
- The customer can filter orders by date range.

These criteria help the development team understand the requirements more precisely and provide a basis for testing the completed feature.

4. Collaborate with the Team
Writing user stories is a collaborative process that involves input from the Product Owner, stakeholders, and the development team. While the Product Owner is typically responsible for creating and prioritizing user stories, the development team provides valuable insights into the technical feasibility and effort required to implement the stories. Collaborating ensures that stories are realistic, clear, and aligned with the team's capabilities.

What Is a Product Backlog?

The product backlog is a prioritized list of all the features, enhancements, bug fixes, and technical tasks that need to be completed for the project. It serves as the team's single source of truth, guiding the work that needs to be done in each sprint or iteration. The product backlog is dynamic and continuously evolving as new requirements emerge, priorities shift, and feedback is received.

The product backlog is owned by the **Product Owner**, who is responsible for ensuring that it is well-maintained, organized, and prioritized. The backlog contains everything the team needs to work on, from user stories to technical tasks, but it is the Product Owner's job to decide what should be tackled first based on the value it delivers to the customer.

Prioritizing the Backlog

One of the most critical aspects of backlog management is prioritization. The product backlog can contain dozens or even hundreds of items, but not all of them are equally important. The Product Owner must continuously prioritize the backlog to ensure that the team is always working on the most valuable features.

Common techniques for prioritizing the backlog include:

1. MoSCoW Prioritization
The MoSCoW method classifies items into four categories:

- **Must have:** Essential items that must be delivered for the product to be viable.
- **Should have:** Important items that should be included, but the product can function without them.

- **Could have:** Desirable features that would be nice to include if time allows.
- **Won't have (for now):** Features that are not a priority and may be considered in the future.

This method helps the team focus on delivering essential features first, while keeping lower-priority items on the radar for future sprints.

2. Value vs. Effort
Another popular prioritization technique involves evaluating each item based on its value to the user and the effort required to implement it. Items that deliver high value with low effort should be prioritized, as they provide the most significant return on investment. Items with high effort and low value may be deprioritized or removed from the backlog.

3. Cost of Delay
Cost of delay is a technique used to assess the impact of delaying a particular item. Features that have a high cost of delay—meaning the longer they are delayed, the greater the negative impact—should be prioritized. For example, if a critical feature is needed to meet a regulatory deadline, the cost of delay would be high, and the feature should be prioritized.

Refining the Backlog

Backlog refinement, also known as backlog grooming, is the process of reviewing and updating the backlog regularly to ensure that it remains well-organized and prioritized. The Product Owner, along with the development team, typically conducts backlog refinement sessions at regular intervals.

During these sessions, the team:

- Clarifies user stories, ensuring they are well-understood and actionable.
- Breaks down large stories into smaller, more manageable tasks.
- Estimates the effort required to complete each item.
- Re-prioritizes items based on new information or changing business needs.

Regular backlog refinement ensures that the backlog stays up-to-date, allowing the team to focus on the highest-priority items during each sprint.

Estimating User Stories

Accurate estimation is essential for effective backlog management, as it helps the team plan their work and set realistic expectations for what can be achieved in a sprint. Agile teams often use techniques like **story points** or **t-shirt sizing** to estimate the relative size and complexity of user stories.

1. Story Points
Story points are a popular method for estimating the

effort required to complete a user story. Instead of estimating in hours, the team assigns a numerical value (often using Fibonacci sequence numbers) to represent the complexity, risk, and amount of work involved. For example:

- A story with 1 point is very simple and straightforward.
- A story with 5 points is moderately complex.
- A story with 13 points is highly complex and may require significant effort.

Story points allow the team to focus on relative effort rather than absolute time, making it easier to compare the difficulty of different stories.

2. T-Shirt Sizing
T-shirt sizing is a simpler method of estimation that categorizes user stories into sizes like XS, S, M, L, and XL based on their complexity. This method is often used for initial estimation when detailed information is not yet available.

Managing the Sprint Backlog

Once the highest-priority user stories are selected for a sprint, they become part of the **sprint backlog**. The sprint backlog is a subset of the product backlog, containing the items the team has committed to completing during the current sprint. The team uses the sprint backlog to track progress and ensure that they are delivering the planned features within the sprint.

The sprint backlog is a living document, meaning it can evolve as the sprint progresses. If new information arises or priorities shift, the team may adjust the sprint backlog accordingly. However, changes should be carefully managed to avoid disrupting the sprint's focus.

Conclusion

User stories and backlog management are the backbone of Agile project management. By writing clear, value-driven user stories and effectively managing the product backlog, Agile teams can stay focused, adaptable, and aligned with customer needs.

Chapter 7: Sprint Planning and Execution

Sprint planning and execution are essential components of the Agile process. These practices help teams align on goals, identify the work to be done, and ensure progress toward delivering a usable product increment by the end of each sprint. Proper sprint planning lays the foundation for a successful sprint, while effective execution ensures the team stays on track, addresses challenges, and delivers valuable outcomes.

In this chapter, we will explore the intricacies of sprint planning, the roles involved, how the sprint backlog is created, and strategies for successful sprint execution.

What Is Sprint Planning?

Sprint planning is the process that kicks off every sprint in an Agile project. It involves the entire team, including the Product Owner, Scrum Master, and development team members. The primary objective of sprint planning is to define the sprint goal and determine the set of user stories or tasks that the team will work on during the upcoming sprint.

The sprint planning meeting usually happens at the beginning of the sprint and typically lasts between 2 to 4 hours, depending on the sprint's length and the complexity of the tasks. The key outcomes of the meeting include:

1. A clearly defined **sprint goal**.
2. A **sprint backlog**, which contains all the tasks the team has committed to completing during the sprint.
3. A shared understanding of the priorities, effort estimates, and the work breakdown for the sprint.

The Roles in Sprint Planning

During the sprint planning session, each team member plays a specific role:

1. The Product Owner
The Product Owner is responsible for presenting the most critical and prioritized user stories from the product backlog. Their job is to explain each story in detail, clarify any questions, and help the team understand the value that each story delivers. The Product Owner also provides context for the sprint goal and how it aligns with the overall project objectives.

2. The Scrum Master
The Scrum Master facilitates the sprint planning meeting, ensuring that it stays on track, follows the Agile process, and respects time limits. They guide the discussion to ensure the team focuses on achievable goals, helps address any roadblocks, and ensures that

team members stay aligned throughout the planning session.

3. The Development Team

The development team is responsible for reviewing the proposed user stories, asking questions, and committing to the work they believe they can complete within the sprint. They also break down larger stories into smaller, actionable tasks, estimate the effort required, and ensure that the workload is realistic given the time and resources available.

Defining the Sprint Goal

A sprint goal provides the team with a shared purpose for the sprint. It is a concise statement that captures the essence of what the team aims to achieve by the end of the sprint. The sprint goal should align with the broader project objectives and provide a sense of direction for the team. For example, a sprint goal might be:

"Enable users to log in via social media accounts."

This sprint goal is clear and focused, helping the team understand what success looks like at the end of the sprint. While individual tasks and user stories will contribute to this goal, the sprint goal ensures that the team remains aligned and understands the overarching purpose of their work.

Creating the Sprint Backlog

The sprint backlog is a list of user stories, tasks, and technical work that the team commits to completing during the sprint. The sprint backlog is a subset of the product backlog, meaning it only contains the items that the team will focus on during that specific sprint.

Here's how the sprint backlog is created:

1. **Reviewing the Product Backlog**
   The Product Owner presents the top-priority user stories from the product backlog, which have been prioritized based on business value and customer needs. The team discusses these stories to ensure everyone understands the requirements and expectations.
2. **Breaking Down Stories into Tasks**
   Once the team has a clear understanding of the user stories, they break them down into smaller tasks. These tasks are specific actions that need to be completed to fulfill the requirements of the user story. Breaking stories into tasks makes it easier for the team to estimate the effort and track progress.

For example, if the user story is "As a user, I want to reset my password via email," the associated tasks might include:

- Design the password reset form.
- Implement backend logic to generate and send reset tokens.
- Create the email template for the password reset notification.
- Test the password reset functionality.

3. **Estimating Effort**
   The development team estimates the effort required to complete each task. This can be done using story points, hours, or other estimation techniques. The goal is to ensure that the total estimated effort fits within the team's capacity for the sprint. Capacity is determined based on the team's availability, taking into account any vacations, meetings, or other commitments that might affect productivity.
4. **Finalizing the Sprint Backlog**
   Once the team has estimated the tasks, they review the total workload and decide if it is realistic to complete within the sprint. If necessary, they may negotiate with the Product Owner to remove or adjust stories to ensure the workload is manageable. The final sprint backlog is then committed to, and the team can begin execution.

Sprint Execution

After sprint planning is complete and the sprint backlog is finalized, the team moves into the execution phase. The goal of sprint execution is to complete the tasks in the sprint backlog while continuously delivering working software or product increments.

Key elements of successful sprint execution include:

1. Daily Standups
During the sprint, the team holds **daily standup meetings** (also known as daily scrums). These short, time-boxed meetings (usually 15 minutes) allow the team to sync up on progress, identify any blockers, and adjust plans as needed. In the daily standup, each team member typically answers three key questions:

- What did I do yesterday?
- What will I do today?
- Are there any blockers or impediments in my way?

Daily standups help the team maintain transparency and ensure that everyone is aligned on progress and priorities.

2. Continuous Collaboration
Sprint execution relies heavily on team collaboration. Agile emphasizes cross-functional teamwork, so developers, testers, designers, and other roles work

together to complete user stories. Communication is key to resolving issues, making decisions, and ensuring that the team stays on track.

3. Addressing Impediments
Inevitably, challenges or roadblocks (known as impediments) arise during sprint execution. It's the Scrum Master's responsibility to help remove these impediments so the team can remain productive. Whether it's a technical issue, lack of resources, or external dependencies, addressing impediments quickly is crucial to maintaining sprint momentum.

4. Staying Focused on the Sprint Goal
Throughout the sprint, the team should stay focused on the sprint goal. While new requests or distractions may emerge, the team must maintain discipline and avoid taking on additional work outside the sprint backlog. The Product Owner plays a key role in managing stakeholders' expectations and ensuring that the team is not pulled off course.

5. Regular Progress Tracking
During sprint execution, the team tracks its progress using tools like burndown charts or task boards. A **burndown chart** is a visual representation of the work remaining in the sprint, allowing the team to see whether they are on track to complete all tasks. A task board (often a digital tool like Jira or Trello) provides a

clear view of which tasks are in progress, completed, or blocked.

Inspecting and Adapting

One of the key principles of Agile is continuous improvement. During the sprint, the team inspects their progress regularly and adapts as needed. If the team realizes that they are falling behind schedule or certain tasks are taking longer than expected, they may adjust their approach, re-prioritize tasks, or collaborate to find solutions. Agile teams are flexible and able to respond to changing circumstances without compromising the sprint goal.

Conclusion of the Sprint

At the end of the sprint, the team should have a potentially shippable product increment that meets the sprint goal. The sprint concludes with two key events:

1. Sprint Review
In the sprint review, the team demonstrates the completed work to the Product Owner and other stakeholders. The team showcases the features they have built and receives feedback. This feedback is critical for refining future work and ensuring that the team is on track to deliver value to the customer.

2. Sprint Retrospective
The sprint retrospective is an opportunity for the team

to reflect on the sprint and identify ways to improve. The team discusses what went well, what could have been better, and specific actions they can take to enhance future sprints. This continuous improvement mindset helps Agile teams evolve and become more efficient over time.

Conclusion

Sprint planning and execution are fundamental to Agile project management. By setting clear goals, creating a well-defined sprint backlog, and maintaining consistent communication throughout the sprint, teams can deliver valuable product increments while staying responsive to change. In the next chapter, we will explore Agile metrics and tracking, focusing on how teams measure success and use data to drive improvements.

Chapter 8: Daily Stand-ups and Team Collaboration

Agile methodologies thrive on communication and teamwork. One of the core rituals that support these principles is the **daily stand-up meeting**. These short, focused meetings ensure that team members are aligned, informed, and able to swiftly tackle challenges. Alongside this, continuous team collaboration forms the backbone of a productive Agile environment, fostering creativity, efficiency, and accountability.

In this chapter, we will dive into the purpose and structure of daily stand-ups, explore best practices for conducting them, and examine the role of team collaboration in achieving project success.

The Purpose of Daily Stand-ups

Daily stand-ups, also known as daily scrums in Scrum frameworks, are brief meetings held at the same time each day. They typically last no more than 15 minutes and allow team members to update one another on their progress, surface challenges, and maintain alignment. The purpose of a stand-up is threefold:

1. **Synchronize the Team**: Ensure that all team members are on the same page regarding the status of work and the sprint's progress.

2. **Identify and Address Impediments**: Surface any blockers or issues that might hinder progress so they can be addressed promptly.
3. **Reinforce Accountability**: Keep each team member accountable for their tasks and commitments to the sprint goal.

Stand-ups are meant to keep communication flowing without turning into lengthy status updates. Instead of deep-diving into technical discussions, the focus is on providing just enough information to keep everyone informed and on track.

Structure of a Daily Stand-up

While the exact format of daily stand-ups can vary based on the team's needs, the most common approach is for each participant to answer three questions:

1. **What did I do yesterday?**
   This allows team members to share their completed or ongoing work and keep others informed about their contributions to the sprint. This transparency helps everyone understand the project's current state.
2. **What will I do today?**
   This question gives insight into what the team member plans to accomplish in the next 24 hours, which helps set expectations and focus priorities.

3. **Are there any blockers?**
   Blockers, or impediments, are obstacles that prevent the team member from moving forward. Identifying blockers early allows the Scrum Master or other team members to help remove them, ensuring that progress continues smoothly.

The Role of the Scrum Master in Stand-ups

The Scrum Master plays a crucial role in facilitating daily stand-ups. They are responsible for ensuring that the meeting happens on time, stays within its timebox, and remains focused. While the Scrum Master may contribute to the meeting, their primary responsibility is to act as a facilitator rather than a participant.

The Scrum Master also takes note of any blockers mentioned during the stand-up and works to resolve them. Whether it's addressing external dependencies, providing additional resources, or coordinating with stakeholders, the Scrum Master's goal is to remove obstacles that could slow the team down.

Best Practices for Conducting Daily Stand-ups

Though daily stand-ups seem simple, maintaining their effectiveness requires discipline and a set of best practices. Here are some tips to ensure that stand-ups add value to the team:

1. **Timebox the Meeting**
   Stand-ups should never exceed 15 minutes. If the team consistently runs over this time limit, it may be a sign that discussions are becoming too detailed. In such cases, longer discussions should be deferred to a separate meeting, often referred to as a "parking lot" discussion.
2. **Stand Up Physically (If Possible)**
   The term "stand-up" originates from the practice of having participants physically stand during the meeting. Standing helps to keep the meeting short and focused, as people are less likely to ramble or become distracted. Even in virtual settings, maintaining a brisk pace is important to mimic the efficiency of physical stand-ups.
3. **Keep It Relevant**
   The focus should always be on tasks directly related to the sprint goal. Side conversations or unrelated topics should be avoided. If certain issues require deeper discussion, they can be taken offline or addressed in follow-up meetings.
4. **Encourage Participation from Everyone**
   Every team member, regardless of their role, should contribute during the stand-up. This fosters a sense of shared responsibility and ensures that the entire team remains informed.
5. **Focus on Collaboration, Not Reporting**
   Daily stand-ups are not status meetings where team members report their work to a manager.

Instead, they are meant to foster collaboration and open communication. The goal is for team members to inform and help each other, not to be held accountable by a manager or supervisor.

Team Collaboration in Agile

Beyond daily stand-ups, team collaboration is a foundational element of Agile project management. Agile methodologies emphasize cross-functional teams, where individuals with different skills and expertise work closely together to deliver value. Collaboration ensures that teams can address challenges faster, innovate more effectively, and maintain a shared understanding of the project's direction.

Here are some ways to encourage and maintain high levels of collaboration within Agile teams:

1. Cross-Functional Teams

In Agile, teams are typically cross-functional, meaning they include members from different disciplines (e.g., developers, testers, designers, product owners). These diverse skill sets are critical to ensuring that the team can deliver a complete product increment at the end of each sprint. Cross-functional teams reduce the need for handoffs between different departments, which can slow down progress.

Having developers and testers collaborate closely, for example, ensures that testing can happen continuously throughout the sprint, rather than waiting until the end. Designers can work alongside developers to ensure that the product's design and user experience meet expectations.

2. Shared Ownership and Responsibility

Agile teams operate on the principle of **shared ownership**. This means that the entire team is responsible for the success of the project, rather than individuals working in silos. Shared ownership fosters a sense of accountability across the team, and team members are more likely to help one another when issues arise.

For example, if a developer finishes their tasks early, they might step in to assist a tester who is struggling with a complex test case. This sense of shared responsibility ensures that the team works toward the sprint goal collectively, rather than focusing solely on individual tasks.

3. Open and Transparent Communication

Effective collaboration requires open and transparent communication. Agile teams should foster an environment where team members feel comfortable raising concerns, asking for help, and providing feedback. Transparency ensures that issues are addressed early, before they become significant problems.

Daily stand-ups, sprint reviews, and retrospectives are all opportunities for open communication. However, communication should not be limited to these formal meetings. Teams that communicate informally and regularly tend to be more cohesive and productive.

4. Continuous Feedback and Improvement

Agile encourages continuous improvement through regular feedback loops. Feedback can come from multiple sources: stakeholders, customers, or even team members themselves. For example, developers may give feedback to designers on usability issues, or testers may provide feedback on code quality.

In an Agile team, feedback is not seen as criticism but as an opportunity to improve. This mindset creates a culture of continuous learning and adaptation, where the team evolves and refines its processes with each sprint.

5. Tools for Collaboration

Collaboration is also supported by various tools that help teams stay organized and aligned. Tools like Jira, Trello, Slack, or Microsoft Teams allow team members to track tasks, communicate in real time, and share updates. These tools become even more crucial in distributed or remote teams, where in-person collaboration is not possible.

For example, a task board in Jira or Trello provides a visual representation of the team's progress, showing which tasks are in progress, completed, or blocked. Slack or Teams enable quick communication, where team members can ask questions, share files, or provide feedback instantly.

Benefits of Strong Team Collaboration

When teams collaborate effectively, several benefits emerge:

1. **Increased Productivity**: Collaboration helps teams identify and resolve issues quickly, reducing delays and increasing the speed of delivery.
2. **Higher Quality Output**: Collaborative teams leverage the diverse skill sets of their members, which often leads to more innovative solutions and higher-quality deliverables.
3. **Greater Flexibility**: Agile teams that collaborate well are better equipped to adapt to changes in scope, requirements, or priorities.
4. **Improved Morale**: Teams that work well together tend to have higher morale. When team members trust and support one another,

they enjoy their work more and feel a stronger sense of accomplishment.
5. **Better Problem-Solving**: Collaboration encourages diverse perspectives, which often leads to more creative and effective solutions to complex problems.

Conclusion

Daily stand-ups and team collaboration are the glue that holds Agile teams together. Stand-ups ensure that the team remains aligned and focused on the sprint goal, while collaboration fosters innovation, problem-solving, and shared responsibility. When executed effectively, these practices enable Agile teams to deliver high-quality results while adapting to change with confidence.

In the next chapter, we will explore the concept of Agile metrics and tracking, which helps teams measure their progress and continuously improve their performance.

Chapter 9: Measuring Progress and Success

In Agile project management, measuring progress and determining success is crucial for maintaining momentum and ensuring that the team is delivering value. Unlike traditional project management, where success is often measured against fixed timelines and rigid milestones, Agile metrics focus on flexibility, continuous improvement, and customer satisfaction. Agile emphasizes delivering working software in small increments, which allows for frequent assessment of progress.

In this chapter, we'll explore key Agile metrics, how to track progress during sprints, and the different ways to measure the success of a project. These tools enable teams to maintain transparency, adapt to change, and achieve goals with confidence.

The Need for Metrics in Agile

Agile project management relies on metrics not just to track progress but also to encourage continuous improvement. Since Agile teams work in short iterations or sprints, measuring how much work is completed and the quality of the work delivered helps identify areas for improvement. Metrics also provide stakeholders with insights into the team's performance, allowing for informed decision-making.

However, it's important to understand that Agile metrics are not about policing the team. Instead, they are tools to promote transparency, facilitate learning, and ensure that the team is on track to deliver value.

Key Agile Metrics

There are several metrics commonly used in Agile to measure progress and success. These metrics can be divided into two broad categories: **team-level metrics** and **project-level metrics**.

1. Team-Level Metrics

These metrics focus on the productivity and efficiency of the Agile team during a sprint. They help gauge how well the team is functioning and where improvements can be made.

Velocity

Velocity is one of the most commonly used metrics in Agile. It refers to the amount of work a team completes during a sprint, usually measured in story points. Story points are a unit of measurement used to estimate the complexity and effort required to complete a task or user story. By tracking velocity over multiple sprints, teams can predict how much work they can realistically handle in future sprints.

It's important to note that velocity should not be used to compare different teams. Every team has its own way of estimating story points, and therefore velocity is relative. Instead, it should be used to help a team understand its own capacity and plan accordingly.

Burndown and Burnup Charts

Burndown charts visually represent the amount of work left to complete in a sprint. The chart shows time on the x-axis and the remaining work on the y-axis. As tasks are completed, the chart "burns down" toward zero. The goal is for the team to finish all the planned work by the end of the sprint, with the line gradually descending.

Burnup charts, on the other hand, track both the amount of work completed and the total scope of the work. This chart provides a clearer picture of whether the scope is changing during the sprint or if the team is consistently progressing toward the sprint goal. Burnup charts are useful in tracking scope creep, where new tasks or features are added mid-sprint.

Cycle Time

Cycle time measures how long it takes for a task or user story to move from the start of the workflow to completion. By tracking cycle time, teams can identify bottlenecks or inefficiencies in their process. For example, if certain types of tasks consistently take longer to complete, the team can investigate why and take steps to resolve the issue.

Shorter cycle times indicate that the team is delivering value faster, which aligns with Agile's focus on iterative delivery.

Work in Progress (WIP)

Work in Progress refers to the number of tasks or stories currently being worked on by the team. Agile emphasizes limiting WIP to ensure that the team remains focused and can complete tasks efficiently. If too many items are in progress at once, the team may become overwhelmed, leading to delays in delivery.

By keeping WIP under control, teams can improve flow and ensure that tasks move swiftly from start to finish. Kanban teams, in particular, use WIP limits as a way to maintain smooth and steady progress.

2. Project-Level Metrics

These metrics focus on the broader success of the Agile project and are often used to communicate progress to stakeholders and business leaders.

Cumulative Flow Diagram (CFD)

A **Cumulative Flow Diagram** provides a visual representation of the status of all tasks within the project. It shows how many tasks are in progress, completed, or awaiting work at any given time. A stable CFD indicates that the team is maintaining a consistent workflow, while a growing "in progress" section may indicate bottlenecks or challenges that need to be addressed.

CFDs are especially helpful in providing an overview of the project's health and ensuring that work is distributed evenly across the team.

Release Burndown

Release burndown charts are similar to sprint burndown charts but cover a larger time frame. These charts track the progress of the team toward delivering an entire release, which may span multiple sprints. The chart shows how much work remains in the release and helps teams and stakeholders understand whether the project is on track to meet its deadlines.

By tracking release burndown, teams can adjust priorities, add or remove features, or extend timelines if necessary. This flexibility is a key advantage of Agile, as it allows teams to adapt to changing circumstances while still delivering value.

Customer Satisfaction

In Agile, success is ultimately measured by customer satisfaction. Agile teams aim to deliver value frequently and early, which allows customers to provide feedback on working software. By incorporating customer feedback throughout the project, teams can ensure that the final product meets the customer's needs and expectations.

Customer satisfaction can be measured through various methods, including:

- **Surveys**: Direct feedback from users or stakeholders.
- **Net Promoter Score (NPS)**: A measure of how likely customers are to recommend the product to others.
- **User Adoption Metrics**: Tracking how many customers are actively using the product or specific features.

By focusing on customer satisfaction, Agile teams align their work with the ultimate goal of delivering value to users.

ROI (Return on Investment)

Return on Investment is another important metric in Agile, particularly for business leaders and stakeholders. Agile projects focus on delivering value quickly, which means that stakeholders can see early returns on their investment. By delivering working software at the end of each sprint, the team demonstrates tangible progress, allowing stakeholders to assess the value generated by the project.

ROI can be calculated by comparing the cost of the project (in terms of time, resources, and money) with the value generated from the product's release or from customer feedback. Agile's iterative nature often results in higher ROI because it allows teams to pivot or make changes before investing too much into features that may not be valuable.

Defining Success in Agile

Success in Agile is defined by more than just delivering on time and within budget. While these factors are still important, Agile places greater emphasis on the value delivered to the customer, the adaptability of the team, and continuous improvement. Let's look at some of the ways Agile teams define success:

1. Delivering Value

The most important measure of success in Agile is the ability to deliver value. Each sprint should result in a potentially shippable product increment that provides some level of value to the customer. Whether it's a new feature, a bug fix, or an improvement in performance, every increment should bring the product closer to meeting customer needs.

2. Continuous Improvement

Agile teams strive to improve their processes and output with each sprint. This focus on **continuous improvement** is often measured through retrospectives, where the team reflects on what went well and what could be improved. Teams that regularly implement changes based on retrospective feedback are likely to see sustained improvements in their performance.

3. Adaptability

Agile projects often face changing requirements or shifting priorities. Success in Agile is measured by the team's ability to adapt to these changes without losing momentum. Agile teams thrive in environments of uncertainty, and their ability to pivot while still delivering value is a hallmark of successful Agile projects.

4. Stakeholder and Team Satisfaction

Success in Agile is also measured by the satisfaction of both stakeholders and the team. Stakeholders need to feel that their input is valued and that the project is meeting their expectations. Similarly, a happy and motivated team is more likely to perform well.

Maintaining open communication, fostering collaboration, and ensuring that the team is not overburdened contribute to long-term success.

Conclusion

Measuring progress and success in Agile requires a combination of team-level and project-level metrics. Velocity, burndown charts, cycle time, and WIP help track the team's efficiency, while cumulative flow diagrams, release burndown, and customer satisfaction provide insights into the overall health of the project. Ultimately, success in Agile is defined by the value delivered to the customer, the team's ability to adapt, and a culture of continuous improvement.

Chapter 10: Adapting to Change

In an ever-evolving business landscape, the ability to adapt to change is paramount for project success. Agile project management embraces change as a fundamental principle, allowing teams to respond quickly to new information, shifting priorities, and evolving customer needs. This chapter explores how Agile methodologies enable teams to navigate change effectively, the mindset required to embrace change, and practical strategies for fostering adaptability within Agile teams.

The Agile Philosophy on Change

One of the core tenets of Agile project management is its recognition that change is inevitable. Traditional project management often operates under the assumption that requirements will remain stable throughout the project lifecycle, leading to rigid planning and a reluctance to alter the original scope. In contrast, Agile acknowledges that changes can arise at any point and encourages teams to welcome them as opportunities for improvement.

The Agile Manifesto explicitly states that "responding to change over following a plan" is a priority. This shift in mindset allows teams to pivot quickly and make informed decisions based on current circumstances, rather than being tied to a predefined plan that may no longer be relevant.

The Importance of a Growth Mindset

To effectively adapt to change, team members must cultivate a **growth mindset**—a belief that skills and intelligence can be developed through effort and learning. This mindset encourages individuals to embrace challenges, learn from feedback, and see failures as opportunities for growth.

In an Agile environment, a growth mindset fosters:

- **Open Communication**: Team members are encouraged to share their thoughts, ideas, and concerns without fear of judgment. This openness facilitates collaboration and the exchange of diverse perspectives, ultimately leading to better decision-making.
- **Continuous Learning**: Agile teams prioritize ongoing learning through retrospectives and feedback loops. By reflecting on their experiences, teams can identify areas for improvement and adapt their practices accordingly.
- **Experimentation**: A growth mindset promotes a culture of experimentation, where teams feel empowered to try new approaches, test hypotheses, and iterate based on results. This

willingness to experiment enables teams to discover innovative solutions to challenges.

Practical Strategies for Adapting to Change

While the Agile philosophy emphasizes embracing change, it also provides practical strategies to help teams navigate it effectively. Here are several approaches that Agile teams can implement to enhance their adaptability:

1. Incremental Development

Agile methodologies advocate for incremental development, delivering work in small, manageable pieces. This approach allows teams to gather feedback frequently and make adjustments based on user input. By breaking work into smaller increments, teams can respond to changes without derailing the entire project.

For example, instead of delivering a complete product at the end of a long development cycle, an Agile team might release a minimal viable product (MVP) with core functionalities. This early release allows users to provide feedback, which can then inform subsequent iterations.

2. Flexible Planning

While Agile emphasizes planning, it also recognizes the need for flexibility. Agile teams should adopt a rolling wave planning approach, where plans are revisited and adjusted regularly based on new information and insights.

At the beginning of each sprint, teams conduct sprint planning sessions to outline the work they intend to complete. However, if unexpected changes arise during the sprint, teams should be willing to adapt their plans. This flexibility helps ensure that the team remains aligned with the project goals and customer needs.

3. Engaging Stakeholders

Frequent engagement with stakeholders is essential for understanding their evolving needs and expectations. Agile teams should maintain open lines of communication with stakeholders throughout the project, soliciting feedback and involving them in decision-making processes.

Regularly scheduled meetings, such as sprint reviews and demos, provide opportunities for stakeholders to review progress and provide input. By actively involving stakeholders, teams can make informed adjustments that align with the project's objectives.

4. Empowering Teams

Empowered teams are better equipped to adapt to change. Agile emphasizes self-organization, allowing teams to make decisions about how to approach their work. When team members feel ownership over their tasks, they are more likely to respond quickly to changing circumstances and take initiative in finding solutions.

Leaders should foster a culture of trust and autonomy, encouraging team members to experiment, voice their opinions, and collaborate effectively. This empowerment creates a sense of accountability and drives the team to navigate challenges with confidence.

5. Utilizing Retrospectives

Retrospectives play a critical role in helping Agile teams adapt to change. These regular meetings provide a structured space for teams to reflect on their experiences, identify what went well, and pinpoint areas for improvement.

During retrospectives, teams should focus on the following questions:

- What worked well during the sprint?
- What challenges did we face, and how can we overcome them in the future?
- What changes can we implement to enhance our processes?

By actively discussing and addressing these questions, teams can implement actionable improvements that enhance their adaptability in subsequent sprints.

Embracing a Culture of Adaptability

Adapting to change is not just about implementing specific practices; it requires fostering a culture of adaptability within the team and the organization. Here are several principles that can help cultivate this culture:

1. Encourage Open Communication

Establishing an environment where team members feel comfortable sharing their ideas, concerns, and feedback is essential for adaptability. Leaders should actively promote open communication by modeling transparency and encouraging collaboration.

Creating opportunities for informal discussions, brainstorming sessions, and team-building activities can help strengthen relationships and enhance communication among team members.

2. Celebrate Learning

Celebrate successes and failures as opportunities for learning. Recognizing team members who take risks, try new approaches, or share valuable insights fosters a culture that values continuous improvement.

Acknowledging both successful outcomes and lessons learned from failures helps create an environment where team members feel safe to experiment and adapt to changing circumstances.

3. Support Professional Development

Investing in the professional development of team members is vital for fostering adaptability. Encourage team members to pursue training, certifications, and workshops that enhance their skills and knowledge.

By equipping team members with the tools they need to thrive in a dynamic environment, organizations can build a more adaptable workforce.

4. Promote Cross-Functional Collaboration

Encouraging collaboration across different teams and functions can enhance adaptability by bringing diverse perspectives and expertise to the table. Cross-functional teams can tackle challenges more effectively and develop innovative solutions.

Organizations should create opportunities for cross-functional collaboration through joint projects, workshops, and shared goals.

Conclusion

Adapting to change is an integral part of Agile project management, and the ability to embrace change enables teams to thrive in a dynamic environment. By fostering a growth mindset, implementing practical strategies, and cultivating a culture of adaptability, Agile teams can respond to evolving circumstances with confidence.

Chapter 11: Agile Risk Management

Risk management is an essential component of project management, particularly in Agile methodologies, where the focus on adaptability and responsiveness to change can significantly influence how risks are identified, assessed, and mitigated. In an Agile environment, risks can arise from various sources, including changing requirements, technical challenges, team dynamics, and external factors. This chapter explores the principles of Agile risk management, the techniques for identifying and mitigating risks, and the importance of fostering a risk-aware culture within Agile teams.

Understanding Agile Risk Management

Agile risk management is rooted in the Agile philosophy of responding to change and delivering value. Rather than relying on a comprehensive risk management plan created at the project's outset, Agile encourages continuous risk assessment and proactive management throughout the project lifecycle.

The goal of Agile risk management is not to eliminate all risks, which is often impossible, but to identify, assess, and respond to risks in a way that minimizes their impact on project objectives. Agile teams must be vigilant in monitoring risks, as the fast-paced nature of

Agile projects can lead to rapid shifts in the risk landscape.

The Agile Approach to Risk

1. **Embracing Uncertainty**: Agile acknowledges that uncertainty is an inherent part of any project. Instead of fearing change, Agile teams view uncertainty as an opportunity for learning and innovation. This mindset encourages teams to embrace the unknown and adapt their strategies as needed.
2. **Iterative Assessment**: Agile teams conduct regular risk assessments during sprint planning, reviews, and retrospectives. This iterative approach allows teams to continuously evaluate risks, prioritize them based on their potential impact, and adjust their strategies accordingly.
3. **Collaboration**: Agile emphasizes collaboration among team members, stakeholders, and customers. This collaboration is essential for identifying risks, as diverse perspectives can reveal potential issues that may not have been considered by a single individual. Engaging stakeholders in discussions about risks fosters a shared understanding and commitment to addressing them.
4. **Focus on Delivering Value**: Agile teams prioritize delivering value to customers. When assessing risks, teams should consider how risks may

affect the delivery of value. This focus helps teams prioritize risk mitigation efforts that align with project goals and customer needs.

Identifying Risks in Agile Projects

Effective risk management begins with identifying potential risks. Agile teams can employ various techniques to identify risks throughout the project lifecycle:

1. **Brainstorming Sessions**: Teams can hold dedicated brainstorming sessions to identify risks collectively. During these sessions, team members should feel encouraged to voice their concerns, share experiences, and discuss potential threats to project success.
2. **User Story Analysis**: User stories are a critical component of Agile development. When creating user stories, teams should consider the potential risks associated with each story. Analyzing user stories can help teams identify dependencies, technical challenges, and external factors that may impact delivery.
3. **Sprint Retrospectives**: Retrospectives provide an opportunity for teams to reflect on past sprints and discuss what went well and what didn't. This reflection can surface risks that were encountered, as well as potential risks for upcoming sprints.

4. **Stakeholder Feedback**: Engaging stakeholders in discussions about risks can provide valuable insights. Stakeholders often have unique perspectives on potential risks based on their experiences and expectations. Regularly soliciting feedback can help teams identify risks early on.
5. **Historical Data**: Reviewing historical data from previous projects can help teams identify common risks and patterns. By analyzing past projects, teams can anticipate similar risks and take proactive measures to mitigate them in the current project.

Assessing Risks

Once risks have been identified, Agile teams must assess their potential impact and likelihood. Risk assessment involves evaluating the severity of each risk and determining its priority for action. Agile teams can use various techniques to assess risks:

1. **Risk Matrix**: A risk matrix is a visual tool that helps teams categorize risks based on their likelihood of occurrence and potential impact. By plotting risks on a matrix, teams can prioritize them, focusing on high-impact, high-likelihood risks first.
2. **Risk Scoring**: Teams can assign scores to risks based on their likelihood and impact. For

example, a risk with a high likelihood of occurring and a significant impact on the project might receive a high score, prompting the team to address it promptly.
3. **Expert Judgment**: Engaging subject matter experts within the team or organization can provide valuable insights during the risk assessment process. Experts can help evaluate risks based on their knowledge and experience, leading to more informed decisions.
4. **Cost-Benefit Analysis**: Teams can conduct a cost-benefit analysis to determine the feasibility of mitigating a particular risk. By comparing the potential costs of mitigation against the potential impact of the risk, teams can make informed decisions about which risks to prioritize.

Mitigating Risks

Once risks have been assessed and prioritized, Agile teams must develop strategies to mitigate them. Mitigation strategies can vary depending on the nature of the risk, but common approaches include:

1. **Avoidance**: In some cases, teams may find that a risk can be avoided entirely by changing the project scope, approach, or timeline. For example, if a specific technology poses a

significant risk, the team may choose to explore alternative solutions.
2. **Mitigation**: Teams can take proactive steps to reduce the impact or likelihood of a risk occurring. This might involve implementing additional testing, creating contingency plans, or allocating extra resources to a critical task.
3. **Acceptance**: Sometimes, the best course of action is to accept the risk and monitor it closely. This approach is often used for low-impact, low-likelihood risks where the cost of mitigation outweighs the potential consequences.
4. **Transference**: In certain situations, teams may choose to transfer the risk to a third party. This could involve outsourcing a component of the project or purchasing insurance to cover potential losses.

Monitoring and Reviewing Risks

Risk management is an ongoing process that requires continuous monitoring and review. Agile teams should regularly revisit their risk assessments and mitigation strategies throughout the project lifecycle.

1. **Daily Stand-ups**: Daily stand-up meetings provide a platform for team members to share updates on their work and discuss any new risks or challenges. This regular communication helps

teams stay informed about emerging risks and adjust their strategies accordingly.
2. **Sprint Reviews**: At the end of each sprint, teams should review their risk management efforts during sprint reviews. By evaluating the effectiveness of their mitigation strategies, teams can identify lessons learned and make necessary adjustments for future sprints.
3. **Retrospectives**: Retrospectives should include discussions about risk management. Teams should reflect on how well they identified, assessed, and mitigated risks, as well as how they can improve their processes moving forward.
4. **Risk Register**: Maintaining a risk register can help teams track identified risks, their assessments, and mitigation strategies. A risk register serves as a living document that can be updated throughout the project, providing a clear overview of the team's risk management efforts.

Fostering a Risk-Aware Culture

To effectively manage risks, Agile teams must foster a risk-aware culture within the organization. Here are some principles to promote a culture of risk awareness:

1. **Encourage Transparency**: Team members should feel comfortable discussing risks openly without

fear of blame or repercussions. Transparency fosters trust and encourages proactive risk identification.
2. **Promote Accountability**: Empowering team members to take ownership of their tasks and responsibilities fosters accountability. When team members feel responsible for their work, they are more likely to identify and address potential risks.
3. **Provide Training and Resources**: Providing training on risk management practices and tools can equip team members with the knowledge they need to identify and manage risks effectively. Investing in resources that support risk management also demonstrates the organization's commitment to this process.
4. **Celebrate Successes**: Recognizing and celebrating successful risk management efforts reinforces the importance of proactive risk management. Celebrating wins can motivate teams to continue prioritizing risk awareness and mitigation.

Conclusion

Agile risk management is a dynamic and continuous process that enables teams to navigate uncertainty and deliver value to customers. By embracing change, engaging stakeholders, and implementing effective risk identification and mitigation strategies, Agile teams can minimize the impact of risks on project success.

Chapter 12: Stakeholder Engagement

Effective stakeholder engagement is a cornerstone of successful Agile project management. Stakeholders—those who have a vested interest in the project, including customers, team members, management, and other affected parties—play a critical role in shaping project outcomes. Engaging stakeholders effectively ensures that their needs and expectations are understood and met, facilitating smoother project execution and enhancing overall satisfaction. This chapter delves into the importance of stakeholder engagement, strategies for fostering collaboration, and best practices for managing stakeholder relationships in Agile projects.

Understanding Stakeholders in Agile Projects

Stakeholders can be classified into various categories based on their involvement, influence, and interest in the project. Understanding these categories helps Agile teams tailor their engagement strategies:

1. **Primary Stakeholders**: These individuals are directly impacted by the project's outcomes, such as customers and end-users. Their feedback and satisfaction are vital to the project's success.

2. **Secondary Stakeholders**: These stakeholders are indirectly affected by the project, such as other departments or teams that may rely on the project's deliverables.
3. **Key Stakeholders**: These are individuals with significant influence over the project, including executives, sponsors, and decision-makers. Their support and buy-in can significantly impact project success.
4. **External Stakeholders**: This group includes regulatory bodies, suppliers, and partners who may have a stake in the project's outcomes. Engaging external stakeholders is essential for compliance and collaboration.

The Importance of Stakeholder Engagement

Effective stakeholder engagement in Agile projects is crucial for several reasons:

1. **Alignment with Business Goals**: Engaging stakeholders ensures that project objectives align with organizational goals and customer needs. Regular communication with stakeholders helps teams refine their focus and make necessary adjustments.
2. **Enhanced Communication**: Engaging stakeholders fosters open lines of communication, enabling teams to share progress, gather feedback, and address concerns

in real-time. This continuous dialogue is essential for building trust and collaboration.
3. **Informed Decision-Making**: Stakeholders possess valuable insights and knowledge that can inform project decisions. By involving them in discussions, Agile teams can leverage this expertise to enhance their understanding of requirements and potential risks.
4. **Increased Buy-in and Support**: Actively engaging stakeholders creates a sense of ownership and investment in the project. When stakeholders feel heard and valued, they are more likely to support project initiatives and contribute positively to the project's success.
5. **Reduced Resistance to Change**: Stakeholder engagement helps mitigate resistance to change by involving individuals in the decision-making process. When stakeholders understand the rationale behind changes, they are more likely to embrace them.

Strategies for Effective Stakeholder Engagement

To foster meaningful stakeholder engagement in Agile projects, teams can adopt several strategies:

1. **Identify Stakeholders Early**: The first step in effective stakeholder engagement is identifying and mapping stakeholders. Teams should conduct a stakeholder analysis to understand

who the stakeholders are, their interests, and their level of influence.
2. **Establish Clear Communication Channels**: Setting up clear and efficient communication channels is essential for stakeholder engagement. This could include regular meetings, status updates, email newsletters, or collaboration tools. Agile teams should choose communication methods that suit the preferences of their stakeholders.
3. **Involve Stakeholders in the Agile Process**: Actively involving stakeholders in Agile ceremonies—such as sprint planning, reviews, and retrospectives—enhances engagement. This participation allows stakeholders to provide input and feedback, fostering collaboration and transparency.
4. **Conduct Regular Check-ins**: Regular check-ins with stakeholders help maintain alignment and keep them informed about project progress. Agile teams should schedule periodic meetings to discuss updates, gather feedback, and address concerns.
5. **Use Visual Management Tools**: Visual management tools, such as Kanban boards or burn-down charts, can facilitate stakeholder engagement by providing a clear overview of project status. These tools make it easier for stakeholders to track progress and understand project dynamics at a glance.

6. **Be Responsive to Feedback**: Agile teams should actively seek feedback from stakeholders and be responsive to their input. Demonstrating that stakeholder feedback is valued and acted upon fosters trust and encourages further engagement.
7. **Set Clear Expectations**: Clear expectations regarding stakeholder involvement, communication frequency, and decision-making processes can help manage relationships effectively. Agile teams should communicate these expectations to stakeholders at the project's outset.

Managing Stakeholder Relationships

Building and maintaining strong stakeholder relationships is vital for successful project outcomes. Here are some best practices for managing these relationships effectively:

1. **Be Transparent**: Transparency is crucial for building trust with stakeholders. Teams should openly share project challenges, successes, and setbacks. This honesty fosters a collaborative environment where stakeholders feel comfortable sharing their concerns.
2. **Adapt to Stakeholder Needs**: Different stakeholders may have varying needs and preferences regarding engagement. Agile teams

should be flexible and adapt their approaches based on individual stakeholder requirements.
3. **Create Stakeholder Personas**: Developing stakeholder personas can help Agile teams understand the motivations, needs, and challenges of different stakeholders. This understanding enables teams to tailor their engagement strategies and communication styles effectively.
4. **Encourage Two-Way Communication**: Stakeholder engagement should be a two-way street. Agile teams should encourage stakeholders to share their thoughts and ideas while actively listening to their concerns. This collaborative approach enhances relationships and fosters a sense of partnership.
5. **Recognize and Celebrate Contributions**: Acknowledging and celebrating the contributions of stakeholders can enhance engagement. Teams should recognize the support and input of stakeholders throughout the project, reinforcing their value in the process.
6. **Provide Training and Resources**: Providing stakeholders with training and resources can enhance their understanding of Agile methodologies and their role in the project. Educated stakeholders are better equipped to contribute effectively and engage meaningfully.

7. **Be Proactive in Addressing Concerns**: Anticipating and addressing stakeholder concerns before they escalate is essential. Agile teams should remain vigilant and proactively communicate any challenges that may arise, along with proposed solutions.

Tools and Techniques for Stakeholder Engagement

Agile teams can leverage various tools and techniques to enhance stakeholder engagement:

1. **User Story Mapping**: User story mapping is a visual technique that helps teams organize and prioritize user stories based on stakeholder needs. This tool facilitates collaboration and provides stakeholders with a clear understanding of project scope.
2. **Feedback Loops**: Implementing feedback loops, such as regular demos and reviews, allows stakeholders to provide input and see the progress of the project. These feedback mechanisms encourage continuous improvement and alignment with stakeholder expectations.
3. **Surveys and Questionnaires**: Surveys and questionnaires can gather valuable insights from stakeholders regarding their needs and preferences. This data can inform project decisions and enhance engagement strategies.

4. **Workshops and Collaborative Sessions**: Conducting workshops and collaborative sessions with stakeholders can foster creativity and innovation. These interactive sessions provide opportunities for brainstorming and generating ideas.
5. **Stakeholder Communication Plans**: Developing a stakeholder communication plan outlines how and when stakeholders will be engaged throughout the project. This plan should specify communication methods, frequency, and key points of contact.

Conclusion

Effective stakeholder engagement is critical to the success of Agile projects. By fostering open communication, involving stakeholders in the Agile process, and managing relationships proactively, Agile teams can enhance collaboration and alignment with project goals. Engaged stakeholders not only contribute valuable insights but also help create a positive project environment that supports successful outcomes.

Chapter 13: Agile Quality Assurance

Quality assurance (QA) is a critical component of Agile project management, ensuring that products meet the highest standards of quality and that customer needs are consistently fulfilled. Unlike traditional project management approaches, where QA is often a separate phase at the end of the development cycle, Agile integrates quality assurance throughout the entire process. This chapter explores the principles of Agile quality assurance, key practices, roles involved, and techniques for ensuring quality in Agile projects.

The Agile Quality Assurance Philosophy

In Agile, quality assurance is not solely the responsibility of a dedicated QA team; rather, it is a shared responsibility among all team members, including developers, testers, and stakeholders. The Agile philosophy emphasizes that quality should be built into the product from the beginning rather than being inspected in later. Key principles of Agile quality assurance include:

1. **Continuous Quality**: Quality is a continuous process that occurs at every stage of development. Agile teams focus on delivering small, incremental improvements that meet quality standards, ensuring that quality is an ongoing concern.

2. **Collaboration**: Agile quality assurance promotes collaboration among team members, breaking down silos between developers and testers. This collaborative approach enhances communication, encourages shared ownership of quality, and enables quicker identification and resolution of issues.
3. **Customer-Centricity**: Agile teams prioritize customer feedback and requirements, ensuring that the product meets user needs. Quality assurance activities are aligned with customer expectations, and stakeholder involvement is encouraged throughout the process.
4. **Adaptability**: Agile quality assurance is flexible and adaptable to changes in requirements, technology, and team dynamics. Teams continuously assess and adjust their QA practices to enhance quality outcomes.

Key Practices in Agile Quality Assurance

To effectively implement quality assurance in Agile projects, teams can adopt several key practices:

1. **Test-Driven Development (TDD)**: TDD is a software development approach in which tests are written before the actual code. By defining test cases early, developers ensure that the code meets the specified requirements. This practice

helps identify defects before they enter the codebase, enhancing overall quality.

2. **Behavior-Driven Development (BDD)**: BDD extends TDD by focusing on the behavior of the application from the user's perspective. In BDD, teams collaborate with stakeholders to define acceptance criteria and create scenarios that describe how the software should behave. This ensures that the development aligns with user expectations.

3. **Automated Testing**: Automation plays a crucial role in Agile quality assurance. Automated tests can be run frequently, allowing teams to quickly identify defects and ensure that new features do not introduce regressions. Automated testing is especially valuable in Agile environments with frequent iterations and releases.

4. **Continuous Integration and Continuous Delivery (CI/CD)**: CI/CD practices involve regularly integrating code changes into a shared repository and automatically deploying them to production. This approach enables teams to detect issues early, facilitates faster feedback, and supports the rapid delivery of high-quality software.

5. **Peer Reviews and Pair Programming**: Peer reviews and pair programming encourage collaboration and knowledge sharing among team members. By reviewing each other's work, developers can catch defects early and learn

from one another, contributing to improved code quality.
6. **Regular Retrospectives**: Conducting retrospectives allows teams to reflect on their processes and identify areas for improvement. By discussing quality-related challenges and successes, teams can implement changes that enhance their QA practices.
7. **Definition of Done (DoD)**: The Definition of Done is a shared understanding among team members of what it means for a feature or user story to be considered complete. It typically includes criteria related to quality, testing, documentation, and acceptance by stakeholders. Establishing a clear DoD helps ensure that quality standards are met consistently.

Roles in Agile Quality Assurance

In Agile projects, various roles contribute to quality assurance efforts:

1. **Product Owner**: The product owner plays a vital role in defining acceptance criteria and ensuring that user stories meet customer needs. Their involvement helps ensure that quality is aligned with stakeholder expectations.
2. **Developers**: Developers are responsible for writing high-quality code and implementing

tests. They collaborate closely with testers to ensure that features meet defined quality standards.
3. **Testers**: Testers, or QA specialists, focus on validating that the software meets the required standards. They develop test cases, perform testing (both manual and automated), and collaborate with developers to identify and resolve issues.
4. **Scrum Master**: The Scrum Master facilitates Agile processes and removes obstacles that may hinder quality assurance efforts. They help foster a culture of quality within the team and ensure that QA practices are integrated into the development process.
5. **Stakeholders**: Stakeholders, including customers and end-users, provide valuable feedback and insights that inform quality assurance efforts. Their involvement ensures that the product meets user needs and expectations.

Techniques for Ensuring Quality in Agile Projects

Agile teams can utilize various techniques to ensure quality throughout the development process:

1. **Exploratory Testing**: Exploratory testing involves testers actively exploring the application to identify defects without predefined test cases. This approach allows for the discovery of issues

that may not be captured in traditional testing scenarios.
2. **Smoke Testing**: Smoke testing is a preliminary test to check whether the basic functionalities of an application work as expected. It helps identify critical issues before more in-depth testing is conducted.
3. **Regression Testing**: Regression testing ensures that new code changes do not adversely affect existing functionality. This practice is crucial in Agile environments, where frequent changes and iterations occur.
4. **Performance Testing**: Performance testing assesses the responsiveness, stability, and scalability of the application under varying conditions. Agile teams should incorporate performance testing into their processes to ensure that the software meets performance standards.
5. **User Acceptance Testing (UAT)**: UAT involves end-users testing the application to verify that it meets their needs and expectations. Engaging users in this testing phase ensures that the final product is aligned with customer requirements.
6. **Load Testing**: Load testing evaluates how the application performs under expected user loads. This technique helps identify potential bottlenecks and ensures that the application can handle real-world usage scenarios.

7. **Code Quality Analysis**: Implementing code quality analysis tools helps identify potential issues in the codebase, such as security vulnerabilities, code smells, and adherence to coding standards. These tools provide insights into the quality of the code and guide developers in making improvements.

Conclusion

Agile quality assurance is an integral aspect of the Agile project management process, emphasizing collaboration, continuous improvement, and customer-centricity. By embedding quality assurance practices throughout the development cycle, Agile teams can deliver high-quality products that meet customer needs and expectations. Through the adoption of techniques like TDD, automated testing, and continuous integration, teams can enhance their quality assurance efforts and foster a culture of excellence.

Chapter 14: Scaling Agile

As organizations grow and projects become more complex, scaling Agile methodologies becomes essential to maintain efficiency, consistency, and quality across multiple teams and departments. Scaling Agile involves adapting Agile principles and practices to larger teams or multi-team environments, ensuring that Agile values are preserved while accommodating the unique challenges that arise in a scaled setting. This chapter explores the concepts, frameworks, and best practices for effectively scaling Agile within an organization.

Understanding the Need for Scaling Agile

Agile methodologies are primarily designed for small, cross-functional teams that can respond quickly to change and deliver incremental value. However, as organizations expand or take on larger projects, the following challenges can arise:

1. **Coordination Across Teams**: In a multi-team environment, coordinating efforts, aligning priorities, and ensuring effective communication can become challenging. Lack of synchronization may lead to misalignment, duplication of effort, and inefficiencies.
2. **Integration of Work**: As different teams work on various components of a project, integrating their outputs can become complex. Ensuring

that all parts function seamlessly together is essential for delivering a cohesive product.
3. **Consistent Practices**: Scaling Agile often requires maintaining consistency in practices, processes, and standards across multiple teams. Without a common framework, teams may adopt varying interpretations of Agile principles, leading to inconsistencies and confusion.
4. **Stakeholder Engagement**: In larger organizations, engaging stakeholders effectively can become more challenging. Maintaining communication and ensuring that stakeholders' needs are addressed requires careful planning and execution.
5. **Cultural Challenges**: Scaling Agile often involves a cultural shift across the organization. Resistance to change, hierarchical structures, and varying levels of Agile maturity can hinder the successful implementation of scaled Agile practices.

Frameworks for Scaling Agile

Several frameworks have emerged to address the challenges of scaling Agile, each offering its approach and methodologies. Some of the most widely adopted frameworks include:

1. **Scaled Agile Framework (SAFe)**: SAFe provides a structured approach to scaling Agile across large

enterprises. It emphasizes alignment, collaboration, and delivery across multiple teams through defined roles, events, and artifacts. SAFe introduces concepts such as Agile Release Trains (ARTs), which are teams of Agile teams that work together to deliver value incrementally.
2. **Large Scale Scrum (LeSS)**: LeSS expands the Scrum framework to multiple teams working on the same product. It retains the core Scrum principles while providing guidance on scaling through roles, events, and artifacts at the organizational level. LeSS focuses on empirical process control and encourages a simple and transparent approach to scaling.
3. **Disciplined Agile Delivery (DAD)**: DAD is a process decision framework that combines various Agile methodologies and practices. It focuses on delivering value and optimizing processes through a disciplined approach that includes governance, architecture, and lifecycle management. DAD encourages teams to choose the most appropriate practices based on their context and needs.
4. **Nexus**: Nexus is a framework designed to integrate the work of multiple Scrum teams. It introduces a Nexus Integration Team (NIT) responsible for ensuring that the work of all teams is aligned and integrated. Nexus emphasizes transparency and collaboration,

focusing on minimizing dependencies and ensuring consistent delivery.
5. **Spotify Model**: The Spotify Model is an organizational structure developed by Spotify to promote Agile principles at scale. It emphasizes autonomous teams (squads) organized around features or components, tribes that group squads with similar missions, chapters that focus on functional expertise, and guilds that foster community and knowledge sharing across the organization.

Key Principles for Scaling Agile

When scaling Agile within an organization, it is essential to adhere to the following key principles:

1. **Preserve Agile Values**: While adapting Agile practices for larger teams, it is crucial to preserve the core values and principles of the Agile Manifesto. This includes maintaining a focus on customer collaboration, responding to change, and delivering working software frequently.
2. **Foster Collaboration**: Encourage collaboration and communication among teams to ensure alignment and reduce silos. Facilitate regular cross-team meetings, retrospectives, and knowledge-sharing sessions to promote transparency and cooperation.

3. **Empower Teams**: Empower teams to make decisions and take ownership of their work. Encourage self-organization and autonomy, allowing teams to adapt their processes to suit their specific needs while aligning with organizational goals.
4. **Define Clear Roles and Responsibilities**: Clearly define roles and responsibilities for each team and stakeholder involved in the scaled Agile process. This clarity helps prevent confusion and ensures accountability.
5. **Implement a Common Language and Practices**: Establish a common language and set of practices across teams to facilitate effective communication and understanding. This consistency helps streamline collaboration and ensures that everyone is on the same page.
6. **Measure and Reflect**: Continuously measure the effectiveness of scaled Agile practices through metrics, feedback, and retrospectives. Encourage teams to reflect on their performance, learn from experiences, and make adjustments as necessary.

Best Practices for Scaling Agile

To successfully scale Agile, organizations can adopt several best practices:

1. **Establish Agile Governance**: Create an Agile governance framework that outlines decision-making processes, roles, and responsibilities across the organization. This framework helps ensure that Agile principles are upheld while providing structure to support scaling efforts.
2. **Invest in Training and Coaching**: Provide training and coaching for teams and leaders to build Agile capabilities and foster a shared understanding of Agile principles. Empowering individuals with knowledge enhances the overall effectiveness of scaling efforts.
3. **Create Agile Centers of Excellence (CoE)**: Establish Agile CoEs to promote best practices, share knowledge, and support teams in their Agile journeys. These centers can provide resources, training, and guidance to facilitate scaling efforts.
4. **Use Agile Tools and Technologies**: Leverage Agile project management tools that support collaboration, transparency, and integration across teams. These tools can help streamline workflows, facilitate communication, and provide visibility into project status.
5. **Encourage Cross-Functional Collaboration**: Promote cross-functional collaboration among teams by involving diverse skill sets in the development process. This collaboration helps foster innovation and ensures that various perspectives are considered.

6. **Regularly Inspect and Adapt**: Encourage teams to regularly inspect their processes and adapt based on feedback and lessons learned. This iterative approach supports continuous improvement and ensures that scaling efforts remain aligned with organizational goals.

Conclusion

Scaling Agile is a complex yet essential endeavor for organizations seeking to enhance their ability to deliver value in a rapidly changing environment. By leveraging established frameworks, adhering to key principles, and adopting best practices, organizations can effectively navigate the challenges of scaling Agile. Successful scaling not only improves collaboration and efficiency but also fosters a culture of continuous improvement, innovation, and customer-centricity.

Chapter 15: Agile Tools and Technologies

In the fast-paced world of Agile project management, tools and technologies play a crucial role in enhancing team collaboration, streamlining workflows, and ensuring transparency throughout the development process. As Agile principles emphasize flexibility, communication, and continuous improvement, the right set of tools can empower teams to deliver high-quality products efficiently. This chapter explores various Agile tools and technologies, their features, and how they contribute to successful Agile practices.

The Importance of Agile Tools

Agile tools are essential for several reasons:

1. **Facilitating Communication**: Agile methodologies rely heavily on collaboration and communication among team members. Tools that enable real-time communication help teams share information, provide updates, and resolve issues quickly.
2. **Enhancing Visibility**: Agile tools provide visibility into project progress, tasks, and team performance. This transparency allows stakeholders to track the status of work and make informed decisions.

3. **Supporting Iterative Development**: Agile emphasizes incremental delivery and frequent iterations. Tools that support sprint planning, task management, and backlog refinement enable teams to manage their work effectively.
4. **Enabling Remote Collaboration**: As remote work becomes more prevalent, Agile tools that facilitate virtual collaboration become indispensable. These tools allow geographically dispersed teams to work together seamlessly.
5. **Streamlining Processes**: Agile tools help automate repetitive tasks, reduce manual effort, and optimize workflows. This efficiency allows teams to focus on delivering value rather than getting bogged down by administrative tasks.

Types of Agile Tools

Agile tools can be categorized into several types, each serving different purposes within the Agile process:

1. **Project Management Tools**: These tools help teams plan, track, and manage projects effectively. They often include features for backlog management, sprint planning, and progress tracking. Popular project management tools include:
    - **Jira**: A widely used tool for Agile project management, Jira allows teams to create and manage user stories, tasks, and

sprints. Its customizable workflows, reporting features, and integration capabilities make it suitable for various Agile methodologies.
- **Trello**: Trello uses a visual board and card system to help teams organize tasks and projects. Its simplicity and flexibility make it a popular choice for smaller teams or those new to Agile.
- **Asana**: Asana provides a comprehensive project management platform with features for task assignments, deadlines, and progress tracking. It supports Agile practices through customizable workflows and project views.

2. **Collaboration Tools**: Effective collaboration is vital for Agile success, and these tools facilitate communication and teamwork. Some popular collaboration tools include:
    - **Slack**: A messaging platform that enables real-time communication among team members. Slack supports channels for organized discussions, direct messaging, file sharing, and integration with other tools.
    - **Microsoft Teams**: Teams combines chat, video conferencing, and collaboration features in one platform. It allows teams to communicate effectively, share files,

and collaborate on documents in real time.
    - **Zoom**: A video conferencing tool that supports remote meetings, workshops, and stand-ups. Zoom enhances team interaction, allowing members to connect visually regardless of their location.
3. **Documentation and Knowledge Management Tools**: Agile teams need to document processes, share knowledge, and create user stories. Documentation tools include:
    - **Confluence**: A collaborative wiki platform that allows teams to create, share, and organize documentation. Confluence integrates seamlessly with Jira, making it easy to link user stories and documentation.
    - **Notion**: Notion combines note-taking, documentation, and task management in one platform. Its flexibility allows teams to create customized databases and knowledge bases to suit their needs.
4. **Testing and Quality Assurance Tools**: Quality assurance is a critical aspect of Agile, and tools that support testing and QA processes are essential. Some popular tools include:
    - **Selenium**: An open-source testing framework for automating web applications. Selenium supports various

programming languages and is widely used for functional testing.
- **Postman**: A tool for API testing that allows teams to create and run automated tests for APIs. Postman simplifies the testing process and provides valuable insights into API performance.
- **Jest**: A JavaScript testing framework that allows developers to write and run unit tests for their applications. Jest's simplicity and ease of use make it a popular choice among front-end developers.

5. **Continuous Integration and Continuous Delivery (CI/CD) Tools**: These tools automate the process of integrating code changes, running tests, and deploying applications. Some popular CI/CD tools include:
   - **Jenkins**: An open-source automation server that allows teams to build, test, and deploy applications continuously. Jenkins supports various plugins and integrations, making it highly customizable.
   - **GitLab CI**: A built-in CI/CD tool within GitLab that allows teams to automate testing and deployment processes. GitLab CI provides a streamlined

workflow from code commit to production.
- **CircleCI**: A cloud-based CI/CD tool that automates the software development process. CircleCI integrates with popular version control systems and offers a variety of deployment options.

6. **Metrics and Reporting Tools**: Measuring progress and success is crucial for Agile teams. These tools provide insights into team performance and project metrics. Examples include:
    - **Burndown Charts**: Tools like Jira provide burndown charts to visualize work completed versus work remaining in a sprint. This helps teams track their progress and make adjustments as needed.
    - **Cumulative Flow Diagrams (CFD)**: CFDs visualize the flow of work items through different stages, providing insights into bottlenecks and overall team performance. Tools like Kanban boards often include this feature.
    - **Agile Metrics Dashboards**: Tools like Tableau and Power BI can be integrated with Agile project management tools to create customized dashboards for tracking key performance indicators (KPIs) and metrics.

Choosing the Right Tools

Selecting the right Agile tools requires careful consideration of several factors:

1. **Team Size and Composition**: Consider the size of the team and its structure. Smaller teams may benefit from simpler tools, while larger teams may require more comprehensive project management solutions.
2. **Agile Framework**: Different Agile methodologies may have specific tool requirements. Ensure that the chosen tools align with the chosen framework (e.g., Scrum, Kanban, or Lean).
3. **Integration Capabilities**: Look for tools that integrate seamlessly with existing software and workflows. Integration enhances efficiency and reduces the complexity of managing multiple tools.
4. **Usability**: Choose tools that are user-friendly and intuitive. A steep learning curve can hinder adoption and slow down team productivity.
5. **Cost**: Evaluate the cost of tools in relation to their features and the value they provide. Consider both upfront costs and ongoing subscription fees.
6. **Support and Community**: Opt for tools with strong support and an active user community. This can provide valuable resources, troubleshooting assistance, and best practices.

Conclusion

Agile tools and technologies play a vital role in enabling teams to embrace Agile principles and practices effectively. By facilitating communication, enhancing visibility, and supporting iterative development, these tools empower teams to deliver high-quality products that meet customer needs. Understanding the various types of Agile tools available and selecting the right ones for specific team contexts is essential for successful Agile implementation.

Chapter 16: Agile Mindset and Culture

The success of Agile project management extends beyond methodologies, frameworks, and tools; it is deeply rooted in the mindset and culture of an organization. An Agile mindset fosters a culture of collaboration, adaptability, and continuous improvement, enabling teams to respond effectively to changing circumstances and deliver value consistently. This chapter delves into the components of an Agile mindset, the importance of fostering an Agile culture, and strategies for promoting these elements within an organization.

Understanding the Agile Mindset

The Agile mindset is characterized by a set of values and beliefs that prioritize flexibility, collaboration, and customer-centricity. Key components of the Agile mindset include:

1. **Embracing Change**: Agile practitioners view change as an opportunity rather than a threat. This perspective enables teams to adapt quickly to evolving requirements, customer feedback, and market dynamics. Embracing change involves cultivating a willingness to experiment, learn from failures, and pivot when necessary.

2. **Value-Driven Focus**: At the heart of the Agile mindset is a focus on delivering value to customers. Teams prioritize work that has the highest impact on customer satisfaction and organizational goals. This value-driven approach ensures that efforts are aligned with customer needs, driving meaningful outcomes.
3. **Collaboration and Empowerment**: Agile teams thrive on collaboration and self-organization. An Agile mindset encourages open communication, mutual respect, and shared ownership among team members. Empowering individuals to make decisions fosters creativity and innovation, leading to better problem-solving.
4. **Continuous Improvement**: The Agile mindset embraces a culture of continuous improvement, where teams regularly reflect on their processes, outcomes, and interactions. This commitment to learning encourages experimentation and adaptation, enabling teams to enhance their performance over time.
5. **Customer Collaboration**: Agile emphasizes direct collaboration with customers throughout the development process. Engaging customers in feedback loops and involving them in decision-making ensures that the delivered product aligns with their expectations.

The Importance of Agile Culture

While the Agile mindset is essential, it must be supported by an organizational culture that encourages and reinforces Agile principles. An Agile culture is characterized by:

1. **Trust and Transparency**: An Agile culture thrives on trust among team members, stakeholders, and leadership. Transparency in communication and decision-making fosters an environment where individuals feel safe to express ideas, share feedback, and take risks.
2. **Psychological Safety**: Creating a psychologically safe environment is critical for encouraging innovation and collaboration. Team members should feel comfortable sharing their thoughts, asking questions, and admitting mistakes without fear of judgment or repercussion.
3. **Adaptive Leadership**: Agile cultures benefit from leaders who embody Agile principles and serve as role models for their teams. Adaptive leaders encourage collaboration, support self-organization, and prioritize the development of their team members.
4. **Cross-Functional Teams**: Agile culture promotes the formation of cross-functional teams that bring together diverse skills and perspectives. These teams are better equipped to address

complex challenges and deliver comprehensive solutions.
5. **Celebrating Success and Learning from Failure**: In an Agile culture, success is celebrated, and failures are viewed as learning opportunities. Teams are encouraged to reflect on their experiences, extract valuable insights, and apply those lessons to future work.

Strategies for Fostering an Agile Mindset and Culture

To cultivate an Agile mindset and culture within an organization, consider the following strategies:

1. **Leadership Commitment**: Leadership plays a pivotal role in shaping the Agile culture. Leaders should openly advocate for Agile principles, provide support for Agile initiatives, and actively participate in Agile practices.
2. **Training and Education**: Invest in training programs that promote Agile values, practices, and mindsets. Workshops, seminars, and coaching sessions can help teams understand Agile principles and how to apply them effectively.
3. **Encourage Experimentation**: Create an environment that encourages experimentation and innovation. Allow teams to explore new ideas, pilot new processes, and learn from both successes and failures.

4. **Facilitate Open Communication**: Foster open communication channels across the organization. Regular check-ins, team meetings, and feedback sessions promote collaboration and transparency, allowing team members to voice their thoughts and ideas.
5. **Implement Agile Practices**: Introduce Agile practices such as daily stand-ups, retrospectives, and backlog refinement sessions. These practices reinforce collaboration, reflection, and continuous improvement.
6. **Recognize and Reward Agile Behaviors**: Recognize and reward behaviors that align with Agile values. Celebrating individuals and teams who exemplify collaboration, adaptability, and a customer-centric focus reinforces the importance of the Agile mindset.
7. **Promote a Customer-Centric Approach**: Encourage teams to engage with customers directly and solicit their feedback throughout the development process. Understanding customer needs and preferences fosters a culture of customer collaboration.
8. **Create a Learning Environment**: Establish a culture of learning by providing opportunities for professional development. Encourage team members to pursue new skills, attend conferences, and share knowledge with their peers.

Overcoming Cultural Barriers

While fostering an Agile mindset and culture is essential, organizations may encounter cultural barriers that hinder progress. Common challenges include:

1. **Resistance to Change**: Employees may resist changes to established processes and practices. Addressing concerns and emphasizing the benefits of Agile can help mitigate resistance.
2. **Siloed Departments**: Traditional organizational structures may lead to siloed departments that hinder collaboration. Breaking down silos and encouraging cross-functional teams can facilitate better communication and cooperation.
3. **Fixed Mindset**: Individuals with a fixed mindset may be reluctant to embrace change or take risks. Encouraging a growth mindset, where individuals view challenges as opportunities for growth, can help shift perspectives.
4. **Hierarchical Structures**: Rigid hierarchies can stifle collaboration and decision-making. Promoting a flatter organizational structure that empowers teams to self-organize can enhance Agile practices.
5. **Short-Term Focus**: Organizations with a short-term focus on immediate results may struggle to adopt Agile principles. Emphasizing long-term value and customer satisfaction can help shift this focus.

Conclusion

An Agile mindset and culture are integral to the success of Agile project management. By fostering an environment that prioritizes collaboration, adaptability, and continuous improvement, organizations can empower teams to deliver value consistently and respond effectively to change. As leaders and team members embrace Agile principles, they create a foundation for innovation and excellence that drives organizational success.

Chapter 17: Case Studies in Agile Project Management

Understanding Agile project management through practical examples can illuminate its principles, benefits, and challenges. This chapter presents a selection of case studies that illustrate successful Agile implementations across various industries. Each case study highlights the unique context, challenges faced, and the outcomes achieved through Agile methodologies, offering valuable insights for organizations looking to adopt or improve their Agile practices.

Case Study 1: Spotify - Agile at Scale

Background: Spotify, the popular music streaming service, is known for its unique Agile culture and organizational structure. With millions of users worldwide, Spotify required an approach that could support rapid innovation and deliver high-quality features quickly.

Challenges: As Spotify grew, it faced challenges related to maintaining agility while scaling its operations. Traditional hierarchical structures often hindered communication and slowed down decision-making.

Agile Implementation: Spotify adopted a model that emphasizes cross-functional teams known as "squads." Each squad functions like a mini-startup, taking full ownership of a specific feature or area of the product. Squads are grouped into "tribes" for coordination and collaboration, ensuring alignment across teams. The company also introduced roles like "chapter leads" and "guild coordinators" to foster knowledge sharing and support individual development.

Outcomes: This model allowed Spotify to maintain agility while scaling operations. Squads can iterate quickly on features, respond to user feedback, and innovate continuously. The emphasis on autonomy and collaboration led to faster development cycles and higher employee satisfaction. Spotify's Agile approach has become a benchmark for organizations looking to scale Agile practices effectively.

Case Study 2: ING Bank - Transforming a Traditional Institution

Background: ING Bank, a multinational banking and financial services corporation, recognized the need to adapt to the rapidly changing financial landscape. The company sought to improve customer experiences, enhance innovation, and respond quickly to market demands.

Challenges: ING faced challenges typical of large organizations, including bureaucratic processes, slow decision-making, and a lack of cross-functional collaboration. The traditional banking model was insufficient to meet the evolving needs of customers.

Agile Implementation: ING undertook a transformation initiative to adopt Agile practices across the organization. The bank formed cross-functional squads that included members from various departments such as marketing, IT, and customer service. These squads were empowered to make decisions, prioritize work based on customer value, and experiment with new ideas.

ING also implemented a "tribe" structure, similar to Spotify, to facilitate collaboration among squads. Regular ceremonies, such as daily stand-ups and retrospectives, were introduced to enhance communication and foster a culture of continuous improvement.

Outcomes: The transformation led to significant improvements in responsiveness and customer satisfaction. ING was able to launch new products and features more quickly and efficiently. Employee engagement increased as teams felt more empowered to contribute to decision-making. The success of the Agile transformation positioned ING as a leader in innovation within the banking industry.

Case Study 3: Lego - Embracing Agile for Innovation

Background: The Lego Group, known for its iconic building blocks, faced challenges in adapting to digital transformations and evolving customer preferences. To remain competitive, Lego sought to enhance its innovation processes.

Challenges: As Lego expanded into digital products and experiences, the company encountered difficulties in coordinating efforts across different teams. The traditional development processes were too slow to keep pace with the rapidly changing market.

Agile Implementation: Lego adopted Agile practices to enhance its innovation capabilities. The company implemented Scrum and Kanban methodologies to improve project management and streamline workflows. Cross-functional teams were established to facilitate collaboration among designers, engineers, and marketers.

Lego emphasized the importance of user feedback in its development processes. Regular user testing and feedback sessions were incorporated to ensure that products met customer expectations.

Outcomes: The Agile approach enabled Lego to innovate more rapidly and effectively. The company successfully launched digital experiences, mobile apps, and online platforms that resonated with customers. By fostering a culture of experimentation and collaboration, Lego strengthened its position in both the physical and digital markets.

Case Study 4: The BBC - Delivering News in an Agile Environment

Background: The British Broadcasting Corporation (BBC) sought to enhance its digital services to provide timely news and content to its audience. The organization needed to adapt quickly to changing consumer behaviors and technological advancements.

Challenges: The traditional media landscape was evolving rapidly, with increased competition from digital platforms. The BBC faced challenges in delivering news content quickly while maintaining high-quality standards.

Agile Implementation: The BBC adopted Agile methodologies to improve its news production processes. Cross-functional teams were formed to work on specific news topics, enabling faster content creation and dissemination. Daily stand-ups and regular retrospectives were introduced to enhance collaboration and address any blockers promptly.

The BBC also embraced user feedback, allowing audiences to participate in shaping content. This user-centric approach helped the organization better understand audience preferences and tailor content accordingly.

Outcomes: The Agile transformation resulted in quicker news delivery, improved content quality, and enhanced audience engagement. The BBC was able to respond promptly to breaking news and emerging trends, solidifying its position as a leading news provider. The emphasis on collaboration and user feedback created a more responsive and adaptive organization.

Case Study 5: Tesla - Innovating in the Automotive Industry

Background: Tesla, the electric vehicle manufacturer, has revolutionized the automotive industry through its innovative approach and commitment to sustainability. To maintain its competitive edge, Tesla needed to streamline its product development processes.

Challenges: The automotive industry is known for lengthy development cycles and complex regulatory environments. Tesla faced challenges in bringing new models to market quickly while adhering to safety and quality standards.

Agile Implementation: Tesla adopted Agile principles in its product development processes, focusing on rapid prototyping and iterative design. The company emphasizes cross-functional collaboration among engineers, designers, and manufacturing teams to accelerate decision-making and innovation.

Tesla encourages a culture of experimentation, allowing teams to test ideas and learn from failures. Regular feedback loops with customers and stakeholders ensure that products align with market demands.

Outcomes: Tesla's Agile approach has resulted in faster development cycles and successful product launches. The company has introduced several new models and features rapidly, maintaining its reputation for innovation. By fostering a culture of adaptability and collaboration, Tesla has positioned itself as a leader in the automotive industry.

Conclusion

These case studies illustrate the diverse applications and benefits of Agile project management across various industries. Each organization faced unique challenges and tailored its Agile implementation to fit its context, resulting in improved responsiveness, innovation, and customer satisfaction. By learning from these examples, organizations can gain valuable insights into the principles and practices of Agile project management, helping them navigate their own journeys toward greater agility and success.

Chapter 18: Common Challenges in Agile Adoption

Adopting Agile project management practices can bring significant benefits, such as increased flexibility, faster delivery, and improved collaboration. However, organizations often encounter various challenges during the adoption process. This chapter explores some of the most common obstacles organizations face when transitioning to Agile methodologies, along with strategies for overcoming these challenges.

1. Resistance to Change

One of the most significant barriers to Agile adoption is resistance to change. Employees and stakeholders accustomed to traditional project management practices may be hesitant to embrace new methodologies. This resistance can stem from fear of the unknown, concerns about job security, or a lack of understanding of Agile principles.

Strategies to Overcome Resistance:

- **Education and Training**: Provide comprehensive training on Agile principles and practices to help employees understand the benefits of Agile. Workshops, seminars, and hands-on training sessions can facilitate this understanding.

- **Involvement in the Process**: Engage employees in the Agile transformation process by involving them in decision-making and implementation planning. When individuals feel they have a say in the changes, they are more likely to support them.
- **Showcase Quick Wins**: Highlight early successes and improvements resulting from Agile practices. Demonstrating tangible benefits can help build momentum and encourage buy-in.

2. Lack of Management Support

Successful Agile adoption requires strong support from leadership. Without commitment from management, Agile initiatives may struggle to gain traction. Leaders who do not understand or believe in Agile may inadvertently create barriers to implementation.

Strategies to Gain Management Support:

- **Educate Leadership**: Provide training and resources for management to understand the value of Agile practices. This can include case studies, success stories, and evidence of improved outcomes.
- **Align Agile with Business Goals**: Clearly articulate how Agile practices align with organizational goals and objectives. Demonstrating how Agile can contribute to

achieving strategic priorities can help garner support.
- **Encourage Role Modeling**: Leaders should embody Agile principles in their behaviors and decision-making. When management demonstrates commitment to Agile, it sets a powerful example for the rest of the organization.

3. Siloed Departments

In many organizations, departments operate in silos, leading to a lack of communication and collaboration. Agile thrives on cross-functional teams and open communication, making silos a significant challenge during adoption.

Strategies to Break Down Silos:

- **Create Cross-Functional Teams**: Form cross-functional teams that bring together individuals from different departments. This encourages collaboration and ensures diverse perspectives are considered.
- **Promote Open Communication**: Foster a culture of open communication by implementing regular check-ins, collaboration tools, and team-building activities. Encourage employees to share information and insights across departments.

- **Recognize Team Contributions**: Acknowledge and reward collaboration and teamwork. Recognizing cross-departmental efforts can motivate employees to break down silos and work together.

4. Inadequate Training and Understanding

Successful Agile adoption requires a deep understanding of Agile principles, practices, and frameworks. Inadequate training can lead to misinterpretations of Agile practices, resulting in ineffective implementation.

Strategies for Effective Training:

- **Tailored Training Programs**: Develop training programs tailored to different roles within the organization. This ensures that all team members understand Agile principles and how they apply to their specific responsibilities.
- **Hands-On Experience**: Encourage hands-on experience with Agile practices through simulations, workshops, and real projects. Practical application reinforces learning and helps individuals understand Agile in action.
- **Ongoing Support**: Provide ongoing support and resources for teams as they implement Agile practices. Access to coaches or mentors can help

address questions and challenges that arise during the transition.

5. Lack of Clear Goals and Metrics

Without clear goals and metrics, Agile adoption can become aimless and ineffective. Teams may struggle to align their efforts with organizational objectives, leading to confusion and frustration.

Strategies to Define Goals and Metrics:

- **Set Clear Objectives**: Establish clear, measurable objectives for Agile adoption. These should align with broader organizational goals and provide direction for teams.
- **Utilize Agile Metrics**: Implement Agile-specific metrics to measure progress and success. Metrics such as velocity, cycle time, and customer satisfaction can provide valuable insights into performance.
- **Regular Reviews and Adjustments**: Conduct regular reviews of goals and metrics to assess progress and make necessary adjustments. This ensures that teams remain focused and aligned with organizational priorities.

6. Insufficient Focus on Culture Change

Agile adoption is not just about implementing new processes; it requires a cultural shift within the organization. A lack of focus on cultural change can hinder the success of Agile initiatives.

Strategies to Foster Cultural Change:

- **Promote Agile Values**: Communicate and reinforce Agile values such as collaboration, transparency, and adaptability throughout the organization. Leaders should exemplify these values in their actions.
- **Encourage Experimentation**: Foster a culture that encourages experimentation and learning from failure. This mindset promotes innovation and supports the iterative nature of Agile.
- **Engage Employees in Cultural Initiatives**: Involve employees in discussions and initiatives focused on cultural change. When individuals feel included in shaping the culture, they are more likely to embrace it.

7. Overemphasis on Tools and Processes

While tools and processes are essential for Agile implementation, an overemphasis on them can detract from the core principles of Agile. Organizations may become too focused on following specific frameworks or using particular tools, losing sight of the underlying values.

Strategies to Balance Tools and Principles:

- **Prioritize Values Over Processes**: Emphasize the importance of Agile values and principles over rigid adherence to specific processes or tools. Encourage teams to adapt practices to fit their unique contexts.
- **Select Tools That Support Collaboration**: Choose tools that enhance collaboration and communication among team members. The right tools should support Agile practices, not dictate them.
- **Encourage Flexibility**: Allow teams to experiment with different practices and tools to find what works best for them. Flexibility fosters innovation and ensures that Agile practices align with team dynamics.

8. Scaling Challenges

For organizations looking to scale Agile practices across multiple teams or departments, challenges can arise in maintaining consistency and coordination. Scaling Agile can be complex and may lead to confusion if not managed effectively.

Strategies for Successful Scaling:

- **Implement Frameworks for Scaling**: Consider adopting established frameworks for scaling Agile, such as SAFe (Scaled Agile Framework) or

LeSS (Large Scale Scrum). These frameworks provide guidance for coordinating multiple teams.
- **Promote Collaboration Across Teams**: Facilitate collaboration between teams through regular cross-team meetings, knowledge-sharing sessions, and joint planning activities. This fosters alignment and supports a unified approach to Agile.
- **Adapt Scaling Approaches to Context**: Recognize that scaling Agile is not a one-size-fits-all solution. Adapt scaling approaches to fit the unique needs and dynamics of the organization.

Conclusion

While Agile project management offers numerous benefits, organizations must navigate various challenges during the adoption process. By understanding these common obstacles and implementing effective strategies to overcome them, organizations can create a supportive environment for Agile practices to thrive. Successful Agile adoption requires a commitment to change, collaboration, and continuous improvement, ultimately leading to enhanced agility and success in delivering value to customers.

In the next chapter, we will explore the future of Agile project management, examining emerging trends and practices that are shaping the Agile landscape.

Chapter 19: The Future of Agile Project Management

As Agile project management continues to evolve, it is reshaping how organizations approach project delivery, team collaboration, and customer engagement. This chapter explores emerging trends, technologies, and practices that are likely to shape the future of Agile project management, offering insights into what organizations can expect as they navigate this dynamic landscape.

1. Increased Emphasis on Hybrid Approaches

Organizations are increasingly recognizing that a one-size-fits-all approach to project management may not be effective. As a result, many are adopting hybrid methodologies that combine Agile practices with traditional project management frameworks. This approach allows organizations to tailor their methodologies based on project requirements, team dynamics, and organizational culture.

Key Aspects of Hybrid Approaches:

- **Flexibility**: Hybrid approaches provide flexibility, allowing teams to adapt practices based on the project's complexity, size, and stakeholder needs.

- **Improved Stakeholder Engagement**: By integrating Agile and traditional methodologies, organizations can enhance stakeholder engagement through regular updates and feedback loops, ensuring alignment throughout the project lifecycle.
- **Broader Applicability**: Hybrid methodologies can be applied to a wider range of projects, including those in highly regulated industries where traditional project management practices may still hold relevance.

2. Greater Focus on Continuous Learning and Improvement

The future of Agile project management will likely see an increased emphasis on continuous learning and improvement. Organizations are recognizing the importance of creating a culture that supports experimentation, innovation, and knowledge sharing.

Key Practices for Continuous Learning:

- **Regular Retrospectives**: Teams will continue to conduct regular retrospectives to reflect on their processes, identify areas for improvement, and implement changes based on lessons learned.
- **Knowledge Sharing Platforms**: Organizations may invest in knowledge-sharing platforms and communities of practice to facilitate the

exchange of insights, experiences, and best practices among teams.
- **Encouraging Innovation**: By fostering a culture of experimentation, organizations can encourage teams to explore new ideas and solutions, leading to improved outcomes and enhanced agility.

3. Integration of Advanced Technologies

The integration of advanced technologies, such as artificial intelligence (AI), machine learning, and automation, will play a significant role in the future of Agile project management. These technologies can enhance various aspects of project management, from planning and execution to monitoring and reporting.

Key Technology Trends:

- **AI-Powered Decision Making**: AI can assist project managers in making data-driven decisions by analyzing historical data, predicting project risks, and providing insights into resource allocation.
- **Automation of Routine Tasks**: Automation tools can help streamline repetitive tasks, such as reporting, scheduling, and progress tracking, allowing teams to focus on higher-value activities.

- **Enhanced Collaboration Tools**: Advanced collaboration tools equipped with AI capabilities can improve communication and collaboration among team members, regardless of their geographical location.

4. Emphasis on Agile Leadership

As organizations embrace Agile practices, there will be a growing recognition of the importance of Agile leadership. Agile leaders play a crucial role in fostering a culture of collaboration, innovation, and adaptability within their teams.

Key Traits of Agile Leaders:

- **Servant Leadership**: Agile leaders prioritize the needs of their teams, supporting them in achieving their goals while fostering an environment of trust and empowerment.
- **Facilitation Skills**: Agile leaders excel at facilitating discussions, encouraging collaboration, and removing impediments that may hinder team progress.
- **Vision and Adaptability**: Agile leaders possess a clear vision for their teams and are adaptable to changing circumstances, guiding their teams through uncertainty and complexity.

5. Expansion of Agile Beyond IT

While Agile originated in the software development sector, its principles and practices are increasingly being adopted in other areas, such as marketing, human resources, and operations. This trend reflects the recognition that Agile methodologies can enhance collaboration and responsiveness across various functions.

Applications of Agile Beyond IT:

- **Agile Marketing**: Marketing teams are adopting Agile practices to respond quickly to market changes, prioritize customer feedback, and deliver campaigns more efficiently.
- **Agile HR**: Human resources departments are embracing Agile to improve talent acquisition, employee engagement, and performance management, focusing on iterative improvements and employee feedback.
- **Agile Operations**: Operational teams are applying Agile principles to streamline processes, enhance supply chain management, and improve overall organizational efficiency.

6. Increased Focus on Customer-Centricity

The future of Agile project management will continue to prioritize customer-centricity, ensuring that organizations deliver value to their customers throughout the project lifecycle. This focus on customer needs will drive organizations to engage more closely with their clients and incorporate feedback into their processes.

Key Customer-Centric Practices:

- **User-Centric Design**: Organizations will prioritize user-centric design principles, ensuring that products and services are developed with the end user in mind.
- **Frequent Feedback Loops**: Regular feedback loops will be established to gather customer insights throughout the project, enabling teams to make data-informed adjustments and enhance customer satisfaction.
- **Value Delivery Focus**: Teams will emphasize delivering value incrementally, ensuring that each iteration of the product meets customer expectations and addresses their needs effectively.

7. Global Collaboration and Remote Work

The rise of remote work and global collaboration has transformed the way Agile teams operate. Organizations are adapting to a distributed workforce, leveraging technology to facilitate communication and collaboration across geographical boundaries.

Key Considerations for Remote Agile Teams:

- **Effective Communication Tools**: The use of robust communication and collaboration tools is essential for remote Agile teams to stay connected, share information, and collaborate effectively.
- **Maintaining Team Cohesion**: Organizations will need to implement strategies to foster team cohesion and collaboration, even when team members are working remotely.
- **Adapting Agile Ceremonies**: Agile ceremonies, such as daily stand-ups and retrospectives, may need to be adapted to suit remote environments, ensuring that teams remain engaged and focused on their goals.

Conclusion

The future of Agile project management is dynamic and full of possibilities. As organizations continue to navigate a rapidly changing landscape, the principles of Agile will remain central to fostering innovation, collaboration, and customer satisfaction. By embracing hybrid approaches, leveraging advanced technologies, and prioritizing continuous learning, organizations can position themselves for success in an increasingly complex and competitive world. As we move forward, the focus on customer-centricity and the importance of

Agile leadership will shape how organizations adapt and thrive in the face of change.

In the final chapter, we will summarize the key takeaways from this book and provide actionable insights for organizations looking to embark on or enhance their Agile journey.

Chapter 20: Conclusion: Navigating Change with Confidence

As we conclude this exploration of Agile project management, it's essential to reflect on the core principles and practices that empower organizations to navigate change with confidence. Agile methodologies offer a robust framework for adapting to an ever-evolving business landscape, emphasizing flexibility, collaboration, and continuous improvement. In this chapter, we will summarize key insights from the book and provide actionable takeaways for organizations seeking to enhance their Agile practices.

Embracing the Agile Mindset

At the heart of Agile project management is the Agile mindset—a fundamental shift in how teams think about work, collaboration, and value delivery. Embracing this mindset means prioritizing adaptability, customer-centricity, and a commitment to learning. Organizations that foster an Agile mindset create an environment where teams feel empowered to experiment, innovate, and respond to changing circumstances with agility.

To cultivate an Agile mindset within your organization:

- Encourage open communication and transparency, allowing team members to share their ideas, concerns, and feedback freely.

- Promote a culture of trust and psychological safety, where employees feel comfortable taking risks and learning from failures.
- Reinforce the importance of continuous learning by investing in training, mentorship, and knowledge-sharing opportunities.

Building Agile Teams

The success of Agile project management relies heavily on the strength of the teams involved. Agile teams are typically cross-functional, composed of individuals with diverse skills and backgrounds who collaborate to deliver value incrementally. Building effective Agile teams requires a focus on team dynamics, roles, and collaboration.

To build high-performing Agile teams:

- Foster a sense of ownership and accountability among team members, empowering them to make decisions and take responsibility for their work.
- Invest in team-building activities that strengthen relationships and enhance collaboration, whether in-person or virtual.
- Ensure clear roles and responsibilities, allowing team members to understand their contributions while also encouraging collaboration across functions.

Continuous Improvement and Adaptation

Agile project management thrives on the principle of continuous improvement. Teams regularly reflect on their processes, outcomes, and performance to identify areas for enhancement. This iterative approach allows organizations to adapt their practices based on real-time feedback and evolving needs.

To implement continuous improvement effectively:

- Conduct regular retrospectives to discuss what worked well, what didn't, and how processes can be improved.
- Encourage teams to experiment with new practices, tools, and methodologies, allowing them to find solutions that best fit their unique contexts.
- Establish metrics to track progress and performance, enabling teams to assess their effectiveness and make informed adjustments.

Engaging Stakeholders and Customers

A crucial aspect of successful Agile project management is the engagement of stakeholders and customers throughout the project lifecycle. Involving stakeholders ensures that their needs and feedback are incorporated into the development process, leading to higher customer satisfaction and better alignment with organizational goals.

To enhance stakeholder engagement:

- Establish regular touchpoints with stakeholders to gather feedback, provide updates, and align expectations.
- Involve customers in the development process through techniques such as user testing, surveys, and focus groups, allowing their insights to inform decision-making.
- Foster a collaborative relationship with stakeholders, encouraging open dialogue and collaboration throughout the project.

Overcoming Challenges in Agile Adoption

While Agile methodologies offer numerous benefits, organizations may face challenges during adoption. Recognizing these obstacles and implementing strategies to address them is vital for successful transformation. Common challenges include resistance to change, lack of management support, and siloed departments.

To overcome these challenges:

- Communicate the benefits of Agile adoption clearly, highlighting how it aligns with organizational goals and improves outcomes.
- Engage leadership in the Agile transformation process, ensuring their support and commitment to fostering a culture of agility.

- Break down silos by promoting cross-functional collaboration and encouraging teams to share information and insights freely.

The Future of Agile Project Management

Looking ahead, the future of Agile project management is bright, with numerous trends shaping its evolution. Organizations will increasingly adopt hybrid methodologies, integrate advanced technologies, and emphasize customer-centricity. The role of Agile leadership will become more critical, guiding teams through the complexities of change and fostering a culture of collaboration and innovation.

As you embark on your Agile journey or continue to refine your existing practices, keep these trends in mind:

- Stay open to hybrid approaches that combine Agile with other methodologies to suit your organizational needs.
- Leverage technology to enhance collaboration, streamline processes, and support data-driven decision-making.
- Prioritize customer engagement and feedback to ensure that your products and services deliver value and meet customer expectations.

Final Thoughts

Navigating change with confidence requires a commitment to embracing Agile principles and practices. By fostering an Agile mindset, building high-performing teams, prioritizing continuous improvement, and engaging stakeholders, organizations can position themselves for success in an increasingly dynamic environment.

As you implement Agile project management in your organization, remember that agility is not just about processes or frameworks; it's about fostering a culture of collaboration, innovation, and responsiveness. By embodying these values, your organization will not only navigate change effectively but thrive in the face of it.

In conclusion, Agile project management is more than a methodology; it is a philosophy that empowers organizations to adapt, innovate, and deliver value to their customers. Embrace the journey of Agile transformation, and you will find that navigating change becomes not just possible but a source of confidence and growth for your organization.